Bottles, Budgets, and Birthplans

What You *Really* Need to Know to Get Ready for Baby

- Prepare for delivery
- Choose a pediatrician
- Baby-proof the house
- Outfit the nursery
- Enjoy your new arrival

KATINA Z. JONES WITH VINCENT IANNELLI, MD

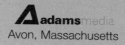
Adams media

Avon, Massachusetts

Published by
Adams Media, a division of F+W Media, Inc.
57 Littlefield Street, Avon, MA 02322. U.S.A.
www.adamsmedia.com

Contains materials adapted and abridged from *The Everything® Get Ready for Baby
Book, 2nd Edition* by Katina Z. Jones, © 2007 by F+W Publications, Inc., ISBN
10: 1-59869-402-2, ISBN 13: 978-1-59869-402-4; and *The Everything® Get Ready
for Baby Book* by Katina Z. Jones, © 1998 by F+W Publications, Inc., ISBN 10:
1-55850-844-9, ISBN 13: 978-1-55850-844-6.

ISBN 10: 1-60550-097-6
ISBN 13: 978-1-60550-097-3
Printed in the United States of America.

J   I   H   G   F   E   D   C   B   A

Library of Congress Cataloging-in-Publication Data
is available from the publisher.

*This book is available at quantity discounts for bulk purchases.
For information, please call 1-800-289-0963.*

Contents

Part 9 • Meeting a New World • 129

Introduction

First of all, congratulations! You are on your way toward welcoming a beautiful new person into the world, expanding your family with the addition of a sweet, curious baby who is sure to brighten your days with each new experience you explore together.

If you're like most parents, you've got lots of questions about your developing little one and the year ahead. How can I plan for my baby's arrival? Should I breastfeed? Will I bond with my baby? Where can I find a playgroup? Are cloth diapers or disposable diapers better? How will I know what to do?

One of the great things about these nine months is that you've got some time to figure it all out! *Bottles, Budgets, and Birthplans: What You Really Need to Know to Get Ready for Baby* is your resource for pregnancy and beyond, answering some of the questions most frequently asked by new parents and offering advice to those for whom this baby may be number two, three . . . or five! It provides 280 tips and tricks—one for each day of your pregnancy—to help you stay informed and get excited for baby's big debut. You'll get ideas for decorating the nursery, tips for finding a great daycare provider you can trust (or determining that you will stay home with your baby), recommendations for choosing a pediatrician, suggestions for how Dad can bond with baby, tricks for giving your post-pregnancy social life a boost, and more.

As parents, embrace your roles with a sense of humor, an open mind—and most importantly—LOTS of love, and get ready for the adventure of your lives! Whether you're singing to your baby in month two, decorating the nursery in month six, getting ready for labor in month nine, or taking your baby to the zoo for the first time, you're building an unbreakable bond with a special being only you and your partner could have brought into the world. Enjoy it!

Part 1

You're Pregnant! Now What?

Once your doctor confirms your pregnancy, you'll likely receive a due date, and then the countdown begins. While nine months sounds like a long time to get ready for your baby's arrival, you'll be surprised at how quickly the time passes. In just three trimesters, you'll have so many decisions to make—from what to name the baby and where to give birth to how, when, and with whom you'll share the baby. You might even need to make some decisions regarding how or when you'll return to work once the baby is born.

There are lots of practical concerns as well. For instance, where in your home will you make room for baby—and how exactly will you decorate the baby's room? How will you go about babyproofing your home, and what changes will you and your husband or partner need to make to your lifestyle in order to be the best parents?

1. *Get Organized*

Once you settle down from your state of euphoria, it's time to start thinking about what you need to do next. Sit down, grab a pen, and start making a to-do list—chances are, once you start telling everyone the good news, you'll be too excited to stay focused on your next steps! To really stay on top of things, make several lists, including Appointments, Calls to Make, Budget Issues, Insurance Policy Review, and Parental Leave Policy Review. Some newly expectant moms even keep a journal with tabs for each of these items so that they can keep a running record of information throughout their pregnancies. This is one of the best ways to stay organized, and it's something you can carry with you to your doctor's office.

2. Take Your Vitamins

Naturally, you'll want to be sure that you're doing everything possible to ensure the healthy development of your baby—starting with making your first doctor's appointment. At (or even before) your first office visit, your doctor will likely tell you to start taking prenatal vitamins immediately. This you will do to help meet the extra nutritional requirements necessary for a healthy pregnancy; also, the folic acid in each vitamin will go a long way toward helping to prevent spina bifida.

mommy info

Be sure to schedule your first appointment with your obstetrician as soon as possible. That way, you can be sure to get a good start on prenatal vitamins—and you can get answers to any questions about what lies ahead in the months leading up to your baby's birth. Come prepared with your list, and take lots of notes.

If you're taking any medications, ask your doctor which are safe to continue taking and which you'll need to either discontinue or modify until after baby's arrival. Don't make any assumptions, especially if this is your first-ever pregnancy.

3. Spread the News Carefully

In the first few days after you learn that you're pregnant, you may be so excited about the news that you want to shout it from rooftops—or tell everyone you see. However, it's often best to wait at least until your pregnancy is confirmed by your doctor. Some expectant moms choose to wait even longer, until the end of the first trimester, since miscarriage rates drop after that time.

Since your doctor and the baby's father are the only other people on the planet besides you who know that you're pregnant in the early days of your first trimester, there's nothing wrong with basking in the glow of your wonderful little secret until you feel ready to announce your good news to the rest of the world. Maybe you can go away for the weekend to celebrate something only the two of you know—or perhaps you can spend some time together making a list of the people in your inner circle who you feel should be told the news in the next day, week, or month.

4. Find Creative Ways to Share

While you can always go the traditional route and simply call everyone on your speed dial to share the news of your impending arrival, it's also fun to share the news in more creative ways. For instance, you might invite all of the new grandparents to dinner at your house, then serve a baby-themed cake for dessert as a surprise. Or create a collage of your own baby photos and print them as a greeting card with a message like, "Guess whose baby . . . is having a baby?" Be creative, and you'll have a memorable keepsake of your early pregnancy days.

5. Compile a Family Medical History

Let your doctor know as soon as you can about any medical conditions that could be hereditary. Create a family medical record that you can update and use in the future as well. Having a good running record of medical conditions and treatment will help both your obstetrician and pediatrician stay informed—and increase the quality of care your family receives both now and in the future. For instance, a family history of food allergies or an allergic-type illness such as hay fever, eczema, or asthma, is important to know about so that you can avoid common allergens while you're pregnant or breastfeeding.

6. Be Prepared for Heirlooms

When you share the news about your baby's impending arrival, don't be surprised if your relatives start offering you lots of items long considered to be part of your family's history. Sometimes they'll offer to lend you actual pieces of furniture such as an antique crib or high chair, while other times it could be clothing or perhaps a baby ring that once belonged to your great-grand-

mommy info

Working on your family tree will not only provide you with important health information, it can also be a great way for you and your partner to learn even more about one another. You'll never have a better excuse to deep dive into each other's family history—and finally answer questions like, "Where'd you get those beautiful eyes?"

mother. Just be sure that any of these family heirlooms is actually safe to use today. In cases where safety cannot be guaranteed, you can still find a way to include such items, even if it's only for decorative purposes.

7. Stay Close to Family

Regardless of your ethnicity, heritage, or spirituality, there are some traditions you may want to create all on your own. For instance, if you haven't been as close as you would like to be with your parents, siblings, or other members of your family, perhaps the occasion of your pregnancy is a good opportunity to reconnect. Perhaps you can host Sunday dinners at your home, or take turns visiting and sharing family stories. If you live far away, it can be a good time to start e-mailing more often, sharing everything from how you're feeling to images from your most recent ultrasound.

8. Create a Pregnancy Journal

You probably can't stop thinking about this incredible little life inside of you: What will she be like? Will the baby look more like you or your partner? Will it be healthy? Questions like these will fill your mind from time to time during this nine-month odyssey.

mommy info

The National Archives (*www.archives.gov*) is an excellent government resource for beginning genealogists, with military, immigration/naturalization, land, and census records dating back as far as 1790. There's even helpful information on how to get started on your search, as well as links to other helpful sites.

The best part about having plenty of time before baby comes is that you also have plenty of time to record your thoughts. A few years from now, when your new baby enters toddlerhood, you can pull out these notes for those inquiring eyes asking you to "tell me about the day I was born"—a moment that most assuredly will come.

9. Write a "Dear Baby" Letter

Write your baby a letter telling her what you looked forward to most after learning you were pregnant. Were you excited, nervous, or giddy? What kinds of thoughts ran through your mind?

Here's an example of a letter you can write:

Dear Baby,

Even though you are not even born today, I feel such a connection to you! When I first found out that I was carrying you, I was so happy—and so surprised! It wasn't always easy, though. I was sick a lot in the beginning, and you were a feisty little thing, twisting and turning. But you should know that you have been loved since the day you were created, and we promise to love you forever.

Love, Mommy

10. Start a Healthy Eating Plan

Remember the food groups you learned about in grade school? Never have you needed them more than when your body is developing a baby. Eat foods from each of the food groups every day. You'll need at least four servings of proteins (such as meat, cheese, eggs, milk, beans, and tofu); at least one vitamin C–filled food (including fruits and vegetables such as grapefruit, oranges, cantaloupe, strawberries, cabbage, cauliflower, and spinach); two or three green leafy vegetables or yellow fruits or vegetables (such as peaches, broccoli, spinach, and yams); four to five servings per day of breads, cereals, and grains (such as whole wheat bread, rice, grain cereal, wheat germ, and pasta). Snack on grapes, apples, nuts, and granola when you can; these foods are easy to pack and carry with you even if you're on the road or at work.

11. Add Smart Calories

You'll need to consume a lot more calories than you used to— but only the good kind, so lay off the chocolate mousse! Simply eating more food than you usually do is not going to cut it; your body needs to have calories with high value—not the empty calories found in cakes, cookies, and pies. You don't have to gain a lot of weight to have a baby, and many doctors prefer that you eat better and weigh less rather than eat everything in sight and

mommy info

Folic acid is an important ingredient in prenatal vitamins recommended by your doctor because it is proven to help prevent neural tube defects in babies. Most of these kinds of defects can be avoided by proper daily amounts of folate in the mother's diet. On their own, most women simply do not consume enough to make a positive difference.

weigh more. Most women gain between twenty-five and thirty pounds during pregnancy. You need only an additional 300 to 500 calories per day for the baby's development. (But see your doctor for advice concerning your own individual requirements, as you may have underlying issues or health problems that require different courses of action.)

12. Remember to Hydrate

You'll need to keep your body hydrated and refreshed, especially with water and milk. Water will flush out any impurities in your system and keep you hydrated. This is particularly important in early pregnancy, when your body is at work cleansing its system in preparation for building a new life. Especially in the last trimester, your milk intake should be three to four glasses per day; this helps your body build calcium levels sufficient for strengthening your baby's bones—with the added benefit of warding off those miserable leg cramps you might be getting. In fact, the leg cramps are nature's way of telling you to consume more calcium.

13. Snack to Keep Nausea at Bay

Small, healthy snacks such as wheat or saltine crackers, granola bars, cheese sticks, oatmeal cookies, raisins, or fruit can help keep your stomach focused on processing food versus creating more nauseating acids. It's a good idea to eat small, high-protein snacks throughout the day even when you're not pregnant, since this is a good way to curb hunger and avoid excess binging. If you eat too much at one time while you're pregnant, your stomach will have a more difficult time processing all that food at once, which could lead to diarrhea, nausea, or even vomiting. If it's still early in your pregnancy and you're having morning sickness, avoid the more acidic fruits, as they tend to upset the stomach.

14. Keep a Food Diary

To stay on top of how much and how well you're eating, one of the best things you can do is keep a food diary. This will not only help you record the number of calories you're consuming, it will also provide a clearer picture of your eating habits, helping you learn where you can improve in order to provide the best "room service" for your growing baby. Share your food diary with your healthcare provider at your monthly appointments, and ask for suggestions or ideas for improvement. For instance, your doctor may recommend restricting certain foods, such as peanuts and peanut butter, if food allergies run in your family.

15. Get in Shape!

If you're like most people, you'll need to take extra care to manage your body during your pregnancy—and long after the baby's born. All pregnant women, especially those in high-risk pregnancies and those who were inactive prior to pregnancy, should speak with their physician about exercise options.

The best forms of exercise are the ones that work your entire body, like swimming, walking, or cycling (as long as you can do it comfortably). Avoid more extreme forms of exercise (like racquetball and marathon running). Low-impact exercise that requires moderate exertion is probably best. Walking, swimming, dancing, and cycling seem to be comfortable and enjoyable activities for most pregnant women.

16. Exercise for a Variety of Benefits

The American College of Obstetricians and Gynecologists (ACOG) recommends pregnant women without health problems or pregnancy complications exercise moderately for thirty minutes or more most days of the week. Exercise helps keep the heart, bones, and mind healthy. Staying active also seems to give some special added paybacks for pregnant women.

- It can ease and prevent aches and pains of pregnancy including constipation, varicose veins, backaches, and exhaustion.
- Exercise may lower the risk of high blood pressure and diabetes during pregnancy.
- Fit women have an easier time getting back to a healthy weight after delivery.
- Regular exercise may improve sleep during pregnancy.
- Staying active can protect your emotional health. Pregnant women who exercise seem to have better self-esteem and a lower risk of depression and anxiety.

17. General Guidelines for Healthy Workouts

According to ACOG, many different types of exercise can be safe for most pregnant women. They recommend following these guidelines when choosing a pregnancy exercise plan:

- Avoid activities in which you can get hit in the abdomen, such as kickboxing, soccer, basketball, or ice hockey.
- Steer clear of activities in which you can fall, such as horseback riding, downhill skiing, and gymnastics.
- Don't exercise on your back after the first trimester. This can put too much pressure on an important vein and limit blood flow to the baby.
- Avoid jerky, bouncing, and high-impact movements. Connective tissues stretch much more easily during pregnancy. So these types of movements put you at risk of joint injury.

18. Squeeze in Some Kegels

Pelvic floor muscle exercises, or Kegel exercises, can help prepare your body for delivery. The pelvic floor muscles support the rectum, vagina, and urethra in the pelvis. Strengthening these muscles by doing Kegel exercises may help you have an easier birth. They will also help you avoid leaking urine during and after pregnancy.

Pelvic muscles are the same ones used to stop the flow of urine.

To do Kegel exercises, simply tighten your pelvic floor muscles for five to ten seconds, then relax for five seconds. Repeat this exercise three times a day, ten to twenty times each repetition. You can do Kegel exercises standing, sitting, or lying down—and no one has to know about it but you.

19. Try to Minimize Stress

Mood swings are, quite thankfully, temporary as the body adjusts to its changes. Crying jags are normal, as are worries about your baby's development and the impending birth experience. Still, you should do everything possible to minimize stress, since it can negatively impact your baby's development and potentially even cause a miscarriage.

There are many ways to help keep stress levels to a minimum. Practicing good stress-management techniques such as yoga,

mommy info

The ancient Chinese relied on a birth calendar to predict the sex of their babies, and many expectant parents still use this method today. It's supposedly 90 percent accurate; however, it's for your entertainment and not to be entirely relied upon as an accurate predictor of your baby's sex.

11

meditation, breathing and relaxation exercises, and even visualization can help you achieve and maintain a sense of emotional equilibrium. Not only that, but they have the added bonus of being able to help you get through labor as well!

20. Get Your Eight Hours

In the beginning of your pregnancy, sleep is not likely to be a problem. But as your pregnancy progresses and the baby begins to grow larger, your sleep cycle may be negatively impacted by the many twists and turns the baby takes!

Change Positions

If it's difficult for you to sleep on your side, try using a full-body pillow and wrap one leg over it to help balance your spine. Or purchase a soft memory-foam mattress that better adjusts to your body's ever-changing shape. Be willing to keep trying different options until you find the one that works for you and helps you get the rest you need for the big job ahead.

21. Build a Support Network

Going through the birth experience alone can be a very difficult experience, both emotionally and physically. Of course, you'll

mommy info

Whether you choose to create a pregnancy journal, time capsule, collage, book, or any other kind of memento to mark your baby's important passage into your lives, this keepsake will become a treasure for many years to come. It's worth the time and effort to make it as complete a history of "time before baby" as possible!

have your partner and other family members or friends in your extensive support network, but who else might you include?

For starters, you should look for a good prenatal or birthing class. Ask family or friends for referrals; your doctor, midwife, or doula may also know of some good classes you both might want to attend. Women's centers at your local hospital are another good resource, as many have excellent health libraries with a number of helpful books, DVDs, videos, or presentations to help you prepare for the big day.

22. Consider Joining an "Expecting Group"

In addition to all of the great online parenting groups and resources out there, you may find it particularly helpful to join an online "expecting group." These support groups are typically composed of other expectant parents either in your geographic area or with the same general due date as you. One of the benefits is that you can go through the entire pregnancy together—sharing tips, problems, solutions, and even emotional issues with one another in a private online forum.

To join an expecting group, go to Google.com or Yahoo.com and use the "Groups" search feature with "expecting group" and your city or due date as keywords.

23. Standard Testing Basics

At the beginning and toward the end of your pregnancy, you may have some pelvic or internal exams. You'll have to produce urine specimens at each visit, and these will be tested for ketones (which may indicate that your body isn't processing food into energy like it should), protein levels (excessive amounts can mean you have toxemia), and glucose (high levels can mean gestational diabetes).

In addition, a urine culture may be done the first month to be sure you're free of bacteria—or at anytime during the pregnancy when the doctor suspects a urinary tract infection.

24. Be Prepared for Glucose Testing

If your urine tests show an elevation in glucose levels, you may have gestational diabetes. A GCT or glucose challenge test will be ordered, and an oral glucose tolerance test (GTT) will follow if the GCT results still show abnormalities. For the glucose challenge, you'll be told to load up on carbohydrates, then report to the doctor's office to drink a glucose solution. An hour later, you'll have some blood drawn and blood serum glucose levels will be checked. The GTT is a more extensive, three-hour fasting test and glucose challenge. If two or more glucose levels are elevated for the three-hour period, you may be diagnosed with gestational diabetes, and your pregnancy will be watched more closely.

25. Take a Peek: Ultrasounds

Not only can an ultrasound give you a first glimpse of your baby, it also shows your doctor where the baby is located (ruling out ectopic or tubal pregnancy) and whether there's enough placenta to sustain the baby comfortably throughout the pregnancy. Your third-trimester ultrasounds will give the doctor a good idea of how large the baby is and whether you'll be able to

mommy info

There are two types of ultrasounds: Transabdominal, which scans over your abdomen, and transvaginal, in which the transducer is inserted into your vagina to produce ultrasonic images of your baby. Transabdominal scans are typically the norm for ultrasounds occurring after the first trimester.

deliver naturally. The doctor may order a level-two ultrasound that provides a more detailed analysis, or you may be sent to a specialist who will perform the test and report the results back to your obstetrician. Remember that you have the right to ask as many questions about the procedure—and why it's being done—as you want.

26. Know the Facts about Amniocentesis

The idea of having a needle inserted into your abdomen to extract some of the amniotic fluid that sustains your baby may do a number on your nerves. Still, having an amniocentesis in the second trimester can be one of the best ways to diagnose chromosomal abnormalities, and it's generally a quick outpatient procedure. Your doctor may order this test if you're older than thirty-five, have a family history of hereditary conditions, are Rh negative, or if there are other medical indications. But as an added bonus, you'll be able to know whether you're having a girl or a boy!

27. Chorionic Villus Sampling (CVS) Can Provide Answers

If chromosomal abnormalities or genetic defects are suspected, or if there are specific genetic conditions your doctor is concerned about being passed on, you may be scheduled for a chorionic villus sampling, or CVS. This test is typically performed in the first trimester (between weeks ten and twelve). Using the ultrasound machine, the doctor will insert a catheter into your placenta, either transcervically (via your cervix) or transabdominally (a needle injected into your abdomen). A small sample of tissue is then taken from placental tissue surrounding the baby. Material from this tissue is genetically identical to your baby's, and can give the doctor a clearer picture of your baby's general state of health.

Part 2

Getting Ready: Childbirth Classes, Nesting, and Names

Your childbirth class will teach you about how to find a group of healthcare providers you feel comfortable with, and during your "nesting" stage, comfort is everything! During this special time, you will want to make the most of the space you will welcome the baby into.

28. Find a Childbirth Class

Ask your obstetrician or call your local hospital to find out where and when childbirth classes are held. Some places charge a nominal fee for these classes; others offer them free of charge. Either way, you need to have some education before embarking on a birthing journey for the first time; it may be called "natural" childbirth, but for first-timers there is often the feeling that nothing is going to happen naturally.

Choosing a class that suits your needs may seem like a daunting task at first; recognize that what's most important is that ultimately you feel comfortable with the teacher and the methods being presented.

29. Know Your Choices

Most good childbirth instructors teach a little bit of all of the childbirth methods, to give first-time parents a good base from which to choose. These methods include:

Lamaze: This method stresses relaxation techniques and conditioning to combat labor pain.

Grantly Dick-Read: The originator of the idea of including fathers, this method relies on a combination of relaxation techniques and mental preparation to get through labor.

The Bradley Method: This childbirth method employs diet and exercise as a sensible way to work through the pain in a medication-free manner.

Whatever method you choose, you should sign up for a class early in order to begin the class no later than your seventh month.

30. Start "Nesting" by Choosing a Nursery Location

Since calm surroundings are so critical to a newborn's development, you should first give some serious thought to the location of the baby's room: Will it be on the same floor as your bedroom? If not, how will you monitor the room—with an audio or video monitor? Will the baby's room be near a busy, noisy street, or will it be facing a backyard where there is nothing but the sound of crickets?

Planning the best location for your baby's room is the starting point in designing the nursery. Once you have decided on the space, then you can begin filling the room with plush toys and cool designs.

31. Choose a Theme

Here are a few of the more traditional themes:

Animals: Kittens, puppies, teddy bears, and farm scenes are typical within this motif, as is a Noah's Ark theme.

Three-ring circus: Clowns, lions, and tigers can fill baby's room with an exciting array of scenes.

Sports teams: If you're a sports-driven family, you can decorate a room in the motif of your favorite team.

mommy info

Before you rush out to choose the décor, write down the room's dimensions; then, when you're at the baby furniture showroom, you'll have a clear idea of what pieces will fit. Such planning will save you infinite amounts of time—and heartache—if the motif you like doesn't fit well within the parameters of the room.

19

Cartoon/TV characters: Licensed characters such as Winnie the Pooh, Mickey Mouse, and Elmo are just a few samples of what's already out there in the baby department.

Pastels: If you want to have a smooth, coordinated look that's a little on the conservative side, solid pastels in trendy shades such as sage, squash, salmon, and lavender might work best for you.

32. Don't Discount Nontraditional Themes

Maybe you don't want the off-the-shelf look of the tried-and-true traditional themes. Here are a few ideas for you:

Suns, moons, and stars: Set your baby's room apart from the rest by painting clouds on the ceiling and hanging fabric moons and stars from it as well.

Fairy tale/storybook: Choose your favorite storybook or fairy tale, and decorate the room with elements that bring the story to life.

African safari: Cultural themes are growing increasingly popular in the new global village. Be creative—for instance, try using pastel shades to paint your "jungle."

Aquatic scene: Use sea-related wall hangings, such as seahorses, seashells, and waves, as a way of adding even more interest to the room.

33. Required Baby Equipment: Start with a Crib

A crib with mattress is one essential item you'll need for your baby. Whatever your taste in crib furniture, try out the floor model to see how easily the side rail comes down. This is an important feature: Look for ease of use and safety for the baby. Most makes and models conform to U.S. standards and carry certification from the Juvenile Product Manufacturers Association (JPMA). In the crib itself, look for the following features: adjustable mattress heights, wheels, and the ability to convert to a toddler bed if that's a function you'd like.

34. Explore Mattress Options

Mattresses for cribs come in foam or innerspring options. They need to fit the crib properly (check dimensions) and should be covered with a waterproof cover. Foam mattresses are lighter and easier to change than innerspring mattresses, and they tend to be more economical. You can also consider fitted sheets, a thin cotton or wool blanket, and dust ruffle.

35. Next on Your List: A Carriage Stroller

Carriage strollers are beautiful but can be heavy. A carriage stroller is defined by the feature of allowing the baby to rest in a flat, horizontal position. Also, the seat is supported by a frame that moves on four wheels. Large, set wheels allow for a smoother ride, and are recommended for mothers planning on lots of walking activities. Carriages set on smaller, swiveling wheels are better suited for quick turns and shopping. Carriage

mommy info

You must have a car seat to take baby home from the hospital, and most states require that babies ride in approved car seats for travel by car or airplane. Remember, the back seat is always safest for your child, and you should never put your baby in the front seat of the car with a passenger-side air bag.

or full-size strollers are recommended for at least the first six months, as the baby will need to fully recline.

36. Another Essential: The *Car Seat*

You have the option of buying a car seat that is strictly for infants (rear-facing only, and handles an infant up to approximately twenty pounds) or one that is for both infants and toddlers (can convert to front-facing once your child is twelve months old and weighs at least twenty pounds; most car seats hold infants or toddlers to forty-five pounds). Also, for baby, you can opt for a rear-facing infant-only seat that doubles as an infant carrier. If it's sheer economy you're going for, however, a combination infant/toddler car seat will probably do the trick.

37. *Stay* in Touch with a Baby Monitor

For centuries, mothers and fathers were able to raise children without these types of products, and let's face it; you should always be close enough to monitor the baby yourself. However, since you can't be everywhere at once, baby monitors really do come in handy, even if just to feel better when your baby is sleeping in another room. If you have portable phones already, make sure the monitor is compatible.

Note that there have occasionally been problems associated with monitors, so it's worth looking into before making a purchase. Check out *Consumer Reports* before buying audio or video monitors. Definitely stay away from used or older models unless you're absolutely certain they're safe—and check for recalls regularly at *www.cpsc.gov*.

38. Recognize What's Optional, Not Required

Sling carriers and backpacks are both optional. Sling carriers keep baby in a good position for breastfeeding and are useful for carrying baby around the house with you as you go about your household duties. You can buy one of these used (and in good condition) at a consignment store, or you can purchase one new and resell it later. If you have a history of back trouble, skip this item.

If you like hiking in the park with baby, the backpack is a terrific product for you. If, on the other hand, your major explorations take place in the mall, it's better to have a carrier that keeps baby in front of you. Backpacks are convenient, yet they can be a little dangerous since baby can't tell you if a branch is about to hit her face. Backpacks cannot be used with newborns.

39. Some Equipment Is Best Borrowed

A swing is a battery- or crank-powered ride that keeps baby in continuous motion. Some babies like them and some don't. You can't really know until you try; so it might be wise to take baby for a test drive. This is a great piece of equipment to borrow.

If you're considering a baby bouncer, stick with the bouncer/saucer variety, which offers baby a view in all directions, yet spins and tilts in one place.

A jumper hangs from a doorway and allows baby to swing or push off the floor. Some children like them; others aren't the least bit interested. The safest ones are those with "bumper guards" that keep baby's body from making contact with the wall.

40. Choose Changing Furniture for Comfort

Some new mothers prefer changing their babies on a table or changing table/dresser combo. You may, on the other hand, feel more comfortable changing baby on a floor mat. Either way, you're going to need a place to store baby's clothes and diaper paraphernalia; so decide which method will work best for you as soon as you can. In the worst-case scenario, if you choose later on not to use a changing table, you'll have a lovely piece of furniture that you can resell later.

41. Think Ahead about Travel

You may want to purchase items that will help your newly expanded family stay mobile. Umbrella strollers are designed for portability. They are completely compact, and fold into themselves for easy storage. These strollers do not typically recline to a flat position. However, they can weigh as little as seven pounds, and are great for traveling. A portacrib is useful for its ability to be transported to Grandma's or to any other visiting spot on baby's busy schedule—and some even function as a bassinet.

mommy info

Talk to other mothers and ask them to share their experiences with you. You might be surprised to find that they, too, worried about whether they might make good mothers. If you don't know any other moms to talk with (or that you feel comfortable enough to talk with), talk with your husband or obstetrician about your dreams. Getting to the heart of your fears as early as possible will help you conquer pregnancy nightmares and leave you feeling better about the new role you are about to take on.

42. Put Together a Basic Layette

For playtime, you'll need five or six undershirts (both full-snap and half-shirt varieties), nightgowns with pull strings at the bottom or a sleepsack, and nonflammable sleepers/rompers with covered feet. You will also need at least four pair of socks or booties (depending on the climate), one sweater or light jacket, two to four waterproof diaper covers (if using reusable diapers), and possibly one snowsuit (again, depending on the climate or the time of year).

For nap or bedtime, you'll need a crib set (including a bumper pad if you choose to use one), three to four fitted sheets, a bassinet sheet (if you're using a bassinet), waterproof crib liners, a light blanket or sheet for cover, a baby roll (for propping baby to sleep on a particular side) if you choose to use one, and a music box or mobile.

43. Don't Forget Bath Time and Changing Time Essentials

For bath time, you'll need a plastic bathtub or tub liner, baby soap, baby shampoo, baby lotion, two to four bath towels (preferably with a hood) or receiving blankets, three to four washcloths, sterile cotton balls, and alcohol (to keep the umbilical cord area clean until it heals).

mommy info

Though your crib set may come with a comforter, it is best not to use it with a newborn for risk of SIDS (sudden infant death syndrome). Instead, use a thin blanket tucked in between the mattress and the crib that goes no higher than baby's chest. Then you can mount that beautiful comforter on the wall as a decorative wall hanging, or use it on the floor for playtime.

For changing time, you'll need to stock your changing table with four or five undershirts or stretchies, petroleum jelly, baby wipes (alcohol free and hypoallergenic), a thermometer, a nasal aspirator, a pair of baby nail scissors, cotton balls and swabs, washcloths, diaper rash ointment, and, of course, hundreds of diapers!

44. Shop for Feeding Basics

You'll need four to six bottles (in both four- and eight-ounce sizes for water, breastmilk, formula, or juice), a bottle brush, a bottle rack (for easy—and sterile—dishwasher cleaning), six to eight bibs and burping cloths, and, if nursing, at least two nursing bras, breast pads, and a breast pump (either manual or electric).

45. Think Ahead: Buy a High Chair

Although you won't need it at first since your baby can't even hold his head up until about three months, you will eventually get lots of use out of your high chair. Your baby does need to be confined during feeding time, and high chairs accomplish this most safely. Plus, there's a tray to protect you from wearing all of the food your baby doesn't take a liking to. The tray will also serve as a "finger food" testing ground for your baby when she's ready to self-feed.

mommy info

Buy toys or mobiles in sharply contrasting colors that are easier on a new-born baby's eyes—black, white, and red work best. The multicolored toys work best when babies are at least three months old and their eyes have had a chance to adjust to the world around them.

46. Wait to See What You Need

One of the most perplexing things about buying things for baby is what to buy and when to buy it. Since you already have your layette in place by now, you should be okay for the first few weeks. What to buy after that time depends on the baby's growth spurts and your financial limitations. Not everyone can afford to buy brand-new clothes every few weeks, and not everyone can afford state-of-the-art baby toys. New or used, be sure you wash all clothing with a gentle laundry detergent before putting it on baby.

47. Save at Consignment Shops

You would do well to shop at consignment stores; most major cities have these, and they are well worth it, since they screen out the worn clothes in favor of the "gently used." There's also the added advantage of being able to return good-quality items for resale to get even more of your money's worth. You could spend $20 to $30 per month on clothes and slightly used toys, but you stand a chance of getting 20 percent back on a resale of the same item.

mommy info

Don't forget to begin reading to your baby from conception on. Invest in a small library of books; often you can find great books at bargain prices at your local library book sales. At first, choose books with simple pictures and few words. Gradually work up to books with simple story lines—especially with rhymes or poetic language.

27

48. Choosing a Name: Start with a List

To get started, create a list of all the important factors you want to consider in choosing a name for your baby. Ask yourself the following questions:

- Is there someone you care about or admire—living or deceased—whom you want your baby to be named after?
- Is there a special place that you might consider using as a name?
- Is there something you're passionate about that would make a great name?
- If you're spiritual, would you prefer a name that reflects your religious heritage?
- How crucial is the meaning of a name in making your selection?

49. Try Out Your Favorites

One way to narrow down your choices is for each of you to keep a running list of name possibilities, and then compare your lists to see which ones are the same. Hopefully, there'll be at least one or two!

After you've created a list of your top ten favorites, practice saying each one out loud to hear how they sound. After all, your

mommy info

Don't make baby naming a free-for-all! To further narrow down your choices, you may want to ask key friends or relatives what they think. But do keep in mind that the more people you involve in the very personal business of naming your child, the more you open yourself up to hurt feelings later on.

child will hear this name directed at him (or her) a thousand times over the next several years; it would be nice if the first, middle, and last names all seem to go together—and don't create open opportunities for teasing by other kids on the playground later on.

50. Get Dad Involved

Many times, amid the monthly obstetrician visits, the baby showers, and all the attention that's paid to the mother-to-be, the prospective father feels a little left out. But there are a few ways Dad can be even more involved in naming the new baby—of course, he'll want to have some choice in the matter!

If you're more concerned about equality, why not let Dad choose baby's first name while you choose the middle name, or vice versa? You can always switch this naming order with your next child! Using this method, you might wind up with some interesting name combinations—but you're sure to have less argument about your final decisions.

51. Be Careful with "Junior"

Some believe that the highest honor you can bestow on another person is to name a newborn baby after him or her.

mommy info

If you are absolutely set on successive naming, note that it is customary to use Jr. when the son is second in line, and Roman numerals for each successive child in the lineage. If baby is the fourth James Smith, his name would read James Smith IV.

29

Although this naming convention can create a great sense of pride for a family, it can also be a problem when Junior grows up. It can create more red tape for government and credit-reporting agencies, as they often confuse one family member's name for another, sometimes with disastrous results. It can also result in mixed-up mail once Junior is out on his own. But more than that, you need to realize that you could be inadvertently forcing baby to live up to the accomplishments of others instead of allowing him an opportunity to develop his own identity in the world. Choose carefully!

52. Organize Names by Category

When it comes to baby names, there are as many possibilities as there are people. One way to wade through the myriad choices is to break them into types or categories of names. For instance, you might create a list of all the old-fashioned names you can think of for both boys and girls, and then create another list that's just ethnic-sounding names you like. Breaking potential baby names into categories like this will help you narrow your choices down even further; if you can hone in on the type of names you like best, your list will instantly become much more manageable—and it'll be easier than ever to zero in on a final selection!

53. Know Which Names Are Popular

Every year, it's a big news story: Which baby names are the most popular in America? If trends and popularity matter to you, or if you simply happen to like some of the names on the "Most Popular" list, go ahead and name your baby from this list. On the plus side, baby won't feel unusual or out of place with other children at school a few years down the road. But on the down-side, nearly everyone else on the playground with the same name will turn their heads whenever a mom or dad calls out.

If you want to use one popular name and one classical one, consider choosing one for your child's middle name. Often unfairly relegated to last-minute thought, middle names offer a golden opportunity for "make-goods" with demanding family members who insist that you bestow upon your baby a name you simply don't like. But you can also use a middle name as a good differentiator between your "Joe Smith" and the thousands of others in the world. Choosing a unique middle name can really help set your child apart in a hurry!

A middle name also offers your child an opportunity to use a first initial and go by a middle name if the original first name is one that he particularly dislikes. Finally, a middle name can be a tiebreaker if you and your mate are deadlocked on two different first-name possibilities. Maybe the middle name should be called The Great Compromise!

The true litmus test of whether you've chosen the right name for your child is to listen to how it all sounds together. For instance, do the first and last names sound melodious, or harsh? How do they sound when you add in the middle name? Listen for cadence and names that seem to roll off the tongue.

mommy info

Use the Web as an idea-generator for baby names. Copy and paste the best options onto a list, and e-mail the list to your family and friends. Or, if you really want to have fun, conduct a name poll on your blog or website. Allow a space for visitors to post and vote on their own name choices.

Also, while it might be tempting and even humorous to name your child "Dow Jones," "Holly Wood," or (gulp) "Frank N. Stein," consider how it will make your child feel later in life when people ask "Is that your real name?" or say, "You're making that up, right?" When it comes to names, you need to think as far down the road as possible in order to head off a lifetime of embarrassment for your child.

54. *Revisit Old-Fashioned Names*

If you're a bit nostalgic and you want a less common name for your baby, you can always choose an old-fashioned name. Old-fashioned names are names that were in vogue 100 or so years ago, but are no longer in the top 100 popular names for babies. Not all of these names are stodgy; in fact, several may even be making a comeback. For girls, some lovely old-fashioned names include Lydia, Clara, Grace, Flora, Lilly, Harriet, Ella, Margaret, Nellie, and Martha. Boys' names that were popular more than a century ago include William, Thomas, Frank, Samuel, David, Herbert, Harold, Edward, Charles, and Henry—and, interestingly, many of these names are still classic choices for baby names.

mommy info

Think twice before you choose names that are difficult to pronounce or spell—and don't get too hung up on a specific unusual name, since your child will likely prefer a more traditional variant later on. For a reality check, imagine your child using your name choice as a teenager or on a driver's license. Keep it real—and manageable!

55. Look to *Other* *Countries* for *Unique* Ideas

Foreign or ethnic-sounding names are becoming more recognizable than ever. If you want a name with the air of the exotic, or simply want to honor your ethnic heritage, an ethnic name might be just the right choice for you and your baby.

Here are just a few ethnic-sounding name options for girls:

- Sophia (Italy)
- Eleni (Greece)
- Matilda (Finland)
- Breana (Scotland)
- Annaliese (Germany)

Ethnic names for boys:

- Moses (Israel)
- Johann (Sweden)
- Anders (Denmark)
- Rashid (Turkey)
- Nicholas (Greece)

Check your family history records first. If you don't find what you're looking for there, visit *www.ellisisland.org* and look up your immigrant relatives. You might be very surprised by what you find on this site.

56. Decide Whether to *Share* Your *Choice*

Whether it's popular or old-fashioned, trendy or ethnic, when the two of you finally do choose a great-sounding name for your baby, the immediate temptation will be to share the news with everyone you know. But many couples are opting to keep their babies' names a secret until the child is actually born. The obvious downside to that is you will have people asking you the same question for months: "So, what's the baby's name going to be?" If you decide to keep the name a surprise, send out a pre-emptive e-mail that tells everyone that you prefer not to be asked that particular question. Or simply reply, "We haven't decided yet." You should be able to keep your "secret name" under wraps until the baby's ready to be born.

57. Plan Your Announcement Strategy

Finally, now that you've chosen a name you both like, it's not too early to start planning for the baby announcements you'll be sending out in a few months. Of course, you can always call everyone immediately after baby's birth, or mail out more traditional-looking printed announcements. The choice is entirely up to you.

Even if you choose to work through your call list on the big day, you'll still want to jot down a little "script" to follow in order to maximize your time. In it, you'll include many of the same details you would on a printed birth announcement: name, birth date, and family members who welcome the child.

mommy info

Generations of parents in every country and of every faith have their own superstitions about what they should or should not name a baby. For instance, a traditional Ashkenazi superstition dictates that if you name a baby after a living person, that person will instantly fall ill and die, since the baby literally took the name's energy; however, Sephardic Jews believe the opposite and honor living relatives by naming a child after them.

If you want to print up personalized birth announcements using your home computer and some preprinted paper, you can set up your template well ahead of baby's birth and fill in the details you already know: Baby's name, birth month and/or year, birthplace, and (of course) parents' and other family members such as grandparents or siblings. That way, when you're ready to head to the hospital for D-day, you'll have one more thing just about done in preparation for baby's world premiere.

When, how, and where to tell the world the name you choose for baby is a personal choice that's ultimately between the two of you. Your family has likely been supporting you emotionally throughout your life, as well as throughout your pregnancy, so show them lots of consideration when it comes to announcing your baby's birth and name! Your parents and siblings should be the first to hear the good news, followed by extended family and friends. Don't let folks in your immediate circle be the last to know; you may regret it later—or worse yet, you may never be able to live it down.

Part 3

Tips for Safety: Babyproofing and First Aid

When you're busy thinking about all the wonderful days ahead in your new life as a parent, the idea that something terrible could happen is the farthest thought from your mind. And while it isn't necessarily healthy for you to go to the opposite extreme—to become consumed with horrible thoughts about your baby's welfare—it is definitely wise to prepare your house and everything in it for the inquisitive young mind about to enter. As far ahead as possible, you'll want to be sure your home is a safe, clean, and happy one for baby—and you!

58. Get on the Floor and Take a Look

Long before your baby's arrival, you should start babyproofing your house in order to make it the safest possible place for your child. But how can you anticipate all of the potentially dangerous situations your little one can face in the obstacle course that is currently your home?

The best way to approach it, besides reading up on baby safety, is to bring it all down to your baby's perspective. Lie down on your floor and take a good look around as though you are your baby. Keep a notebook with you, and make note of anything that's hanging, broken, sharp, heavy, or made of glass. Review the list with your partner, and make sure you deal with each item on your list before the baby comes.

59. Be Aware of the Five Most Common Injuries

For babies, the big, wide world can be an exciting place to explore. Unfortunately, it's also a daily opportunity for injury. According to Safe Kids Worldwide, an international information network focused on preventing accidental injury in children, most of the nearly two million pediatric emergency room visits are due to accidents that occurred at the child's home.

mommy info

You should keep your eyes and ears open for product recall information on car seats, as they tend to happen somewhat frequently. Also, it's a good idea to have your local auto service shop inspect your car seat from time to time, just to make sure it's installed and working properly. Or you can check out www.seatcheck.org, which has an NHTSA car seat safety inspection station locator function (by zip code).

The five most common injuries are: Falls (including things falling onto baby), accidental ingestion/poisoning, drowning (in tubs, swimming pools, or pails of water), burns, and suffocation (mostly in cribs or due to obstruction, e.g., small objects including pieces of food that choked baby).

60. Put Together a Shopping List

Whether or not you need these items depends on the layout of your home and your babyproofing decisions. For example, do you want to latch your kitchen cabinets, or rearrange the contents so that all hazardous and breakable items are stowed high out of reach, and store only child-safe items (pots and pans, Tupperware) in the lower cabinets? A basic babyproofing shopping list should include:

- Outlet covers or caps
- Gates
- Drawer and cabinet latches
- Toilet lock
- Foam strips or corners for table edges
- Window guards
- Window latches
- Oven lock
- Doorknob covers
- Stove knob covers

61. Watch Out for Water

Once baby starts becoming mobile, you'll be surprised how quickly grabbing will begin. You might use doorstops to protect your baby from slamming doors, wall anchors to secure TVs and heavy pieces of furniture, padding for sharp edges on furniture, and stair rails with securely positioned foam pieces.

If you live near a pond or a swimming pool, make sure you keep baby as far away from the water as possible—except if you are swimming together in a shallow pool. If that's the case, then you should definitely use inflatable wings or a life jacket for baby. And never leave a baby unattended in the bathtub—not even for a second!

62. Secure Poisonous Substances

Lock all harmful chemicals (cleaning solutions, medicines, and even some pet supplies) in a babyproof cabinet—preferably one that's up high and out of baby's immediate reach. If baby should get into something potentially dangerous, contact your local poison control center immediately, even if you aren't sure baby actually consumed anything. Better to be safe than sorry—and better yet to avoid potential dangers altogether by keeping as much as you can out of your baby's reach.

63. Don't Forget about Lead and Asbestos

Although a lead-free house is optimal, it can cost as much as $30,000 to de-lead an old house—and the home's architectural detail could be destroyed in the process. If you can't afford to do

mommy info

Never make baby's bath water too hot! Warm water is the safest temperature for baby's bath. Just be sure your hot water heater is set to 120 degrees to avoid accidental scalding. If you don't want to second-guess, purchase a baby bath thermometer and use it until you feel you can safely gauge on your own.

it and don't want to move, a compromise solution is checking frequently to make sure that paint is not peeling (especially on windowsills and ceilings) and remind your pediatrician to have your child's lead level checked routinely.

Asbestos removal can be pricey, but is far less so than lead removal. Asbestos can also be encapsulated for a fraction of the cost of removing it, and that's why many people feel that this alternate option is safe enough for unused, unfinished basements. The choice ultimately depends more on your budget.

64. Select Baby Furniture with Safety in Mind

Parents and caretakers of babies and young children need to be aware of the many potential hazards in their environment— hazards that can occur through the misuse of products or through the use of products that have not been well designed.

Ask yourself these questions: Does your equipment have basic safety features? If not, can missing or unsafe parts be easily replaced with the proper parts? Can breaks or cracks be repaired to give more protection? Can you fix the older equipment without creating a "new" hazard? If you answer no to any of these questions, the item is beyond help and should be discarded. If the item can be repaired, repair it before even thinking of using it.

mommy info

If your parents or in-laws want to pass on an "heirloom" crib to your little one, be sure it meets today's safety standards. Go to the U.S. government's consumer safety website (*www.cpsc.gov*) and download the crib safety checklist. Share it with your parents or in-laws and then brainstorm other creative ideas for the antique piece; perhaps you can use it as a toy display on the other side of baby's room.

65. Examine High Chairs and Hook-On Chairs

Your baby's high chair should have restraining straps that are independent of the tray, which should lock securely. If you have a folding high chair, it should have an effective locking device to keep it from collapsing. Always use restraining straps; otherwise the child can slide under the tray and strangle or fall onto the floor below.

Hook-on chairs are great for visits or a dinner out. Make sure yours has a restraining strap along with a clamp that locks properly onto the table for added security. The caps or plugs on the tubing should be firmly attached and unable to be pulled off by little hands, since they may be a choking hazard. Don't position the chair anywhere the child can push off with his feet.

66. Buy a Safer Toy Chest

Toy chests offer the best opportunity to keep the floor clean in baby's play room—and eliminating opportunities for falls is a good safety precaution. But make sure the lid can't trap your baby, and that any hinged lids can't pinch baby's tiny fingers. The best toy chests for a baby's room are the plastic-molded ones.

Toy boxes should be checked for safety. Use a toy chest with a lid that will stay open in any position when raised, and that won't fall unexpectedly on a child. For extra safety, be sure there

mommy info

Look for and heed age recommendations, such as "not recommended for children under three." Look for other safety labels, including "Flame retardant/Flame resistant" on fabric products and "Washable/hygienic materials" on stuffed toys and dolls.

are ventilation holes for fresh air. Watch for sharp edges that could cut, and hinges that could pinch or squeeze.

67. Check Crib Slats and Sides

On a crib, slats should be spaced no more than 2⅜ inches apart, without any missing or cracked slats. The mattress should fit snugly—less than two fingers' width between the edge of the mattress and the side of the crib—and the mattress support should be securely attached to the headboard and footboard. The corner posts should be no higher than 1/16 inch (1 mm) to prevent entanglement of clothing or other objects worn by baby. Since they can allow head entrapment, there shouldn't be any cutouts in the headboard or footboard. Drop-side latches should securely hold sides in a raised position, and not be moveable by an active or adventuresome baby. When baby reaches 35 inches in height or can climb and/or fall over the sides, it's time for a toddler bed.

68. Consult a Checklist for Used Cribs

Here's what to look for in terms of crib safety:

- No missing, loose, broken, or improperly installed screws, brackets, or other hardware on the crib or the mattress support

mommy info

Protecting children from unsafe toys is the responsibility of everyone. Careful toy selection and proper supervision of children at play is still—and always will be—the best way to protect children from toy-related injuries.

- No more than 2⅜ inches between crib slats, so a baby's body can't fit through the slats
- A firm, snug-fitting mattress so a baby can't get trapped between the mattress and the side of the crib
- No corner posts over 1/16 inch above the end panels (unless they are over 16 inches high for a canopy) so a baby can't catch clothing and strangle
- No cutout areas on the headboard or footboard so a baby's head can't get trapped
- A mattress support that does not easily pull apart from the corner posts so a baby can't get trapped between mattress and crib
- No cracked or peeling paint
- No splinters or rough edges

If your crib doesn't meet these guidelines, you should seriously consider replacing it with a safer one.

69. Do Your Own Safety Checks

To properly maintain toys, check them periodically for breakage and potential hazards.

It is best not to use wooden toys with your baby unless they are smoothly sanded and painted with a nontoxic, protective coating. Just make sure there aren't any splinters. Also, check all

mommy info

Clear the clutter from your home before baby arrives. Get rid of all potentially harmful objects, but also things that you just don't need anymore. Once baby comes, you'll be surprised at how quickly your home fills up with stuff again!

outdoor toys or play areas regularly for rust or weak parts that could become hazardous.

To store toys properly, teach older children to put them safely away on shelves or in a toy chest after playing so that trips and falls can be prevented.

70. Choose Crib Toys Carefully

Parents always want their kids to be occupied—even when they're tucked away in their cribs. But crib toys need to be limited to just a few that are chosen with care, if they have to have any at all. Toys with strings with loops or openings should never be dangling near the crib. If you use a crib gym, remove it when the child is able to pull or push up on her hands and knees or reaches five months of age, whichever comes first. Toys with small components are a choking hazard and should never be left in a crib. Never leave large stuffed animals or pillow-like stuffed toys and other soft products in a crib with a sleeping baby.

71. Watch for Choking Hazards

Pacifiers are great for babies who love to suck on things. But they can also present opportunities for danger. To prevent accidental strangulation, leave off any attachable ribbons until baby is at least six months old. The shield of the pacifier should be large and firm enough to not fit completely into the child's mouth, with ventilation holes so the baby can still breathe freely when it's in her mouth. Throw away any pacifiers whose nipples have holes or tears that might break off into baby's mouth.

72. Choose Appropriate Rattles, Squeeze Toys, and Teethers

Rattles, squeeze toys, and teethers should be large enough so that they can't lodge in a baby's throat. Rattles need to be sturdy enough to prevent breakage during use. Squeeze toys shouldn't contain a detachable squeaker, since these can sometimes be squeezed out of the toy and lead to choking. To prevent suffocation, always remove rattles, squeeze toys, teethers, and other toys from cribs or playpens—especially when baby is sleeping or unattended.

73. Double Check Your Car Seat

Your baby should only ride in a properly installed rear-facing seat that will better protect his or her head, neck, and body from potential impact. The seat should be secured to the vehicle by the safety belts or by the LATCH system (which stands for Lower Anchors and Tethers for Children). If you're not sure whether your car seat is the right one, consult the owner's manual of your car for recommendations and maximum seat dimensions. Also, be sure to thoroughly read the owner's manual that came with the car seat, as it should explain in precise detail how to use the seat properly. Never use the baby's car seat in a front seat where an air bag is present.

74. Let Your Baby Be Safely on the Move

Your baby might enjoy playing in an exercise "saucer" that includes a seat that spins and a rubber disc under baby's feet. These are generally very safe, and lots of fun for active babies. Thankfully, the unsafe, wheel-driven baby walkers of the past are not as readily available, and most experts strongly discourage their use—so politely decline one, even as a hand-me-down.

75. Invest in Baby Gates—Lots of Them

Until babies are old enough to do more exploring on their own, gates are a good way to keep little ones out of areas that aren't childproofed. Gates need to go at both ends of any staircase, as well as in rooms you don't want baby to have easy access to.

Openings in gates should be small enough to avoid entrapping baby's head, with a pressure bar or other fastener that can resist forces exerted by a determined "explorer." To avoid splinters, use plastic-molded gates or expandable enclosures with large v-shaped openings along the top edge or with diamond-shaped openings within.

76. Keep Babyproofing after Your Baby Arrives

Once your child is born and eventually mobile, watch to see what hazards she discovers. Is she fascinated by the oven door? Does she like to throw toys in the toilet? You may want a toilet lock, but since these are difficult for older siblings or uninitiated guests to operate, you may prefer just to keep the bathroom door shut. You may have to strap it closed. Is she climbing the bookshelves? Make sure they are bolted to the wall. Some babies simply require more childproofing than others. You'll soon discover what kind of adventurer lives at your house.

77. Revisit the Kitchen, Family Room, and Home Office

From the moment your baby starts crawling, you'll need to start moving room to room with a fresh set of eyes.

In the kitchen, move all appliance power cords out of baby's reach, and never cook with baby in your arms. In the family room, keep all smaller objects and electronic devices out of baby's reach as well; items like your sewing kit or an older child's toys with small components should never be left out within baby's grasp. Finally, keep your home office off-limits to baby, except for portable cribs or an exercise saucer. There are just too many power cords!

78. Make Bath Time Safe

Bath time should always be a time for caution since, in the water, disaster can strike in a matter of seconds. For any baby bath product, make sure suction cups are securely fastened and that they securely attach to the smooth surface of the tub. Fill the tub only with enough water to cover baby's legs, and never leave baby alone or with a sibling while in the bath ring—even for a second!

Warm water is the safest temperature for baby's bath. Be sure your hot water heater is set to 120 degrees to avoid accidental scalding.

79. Be Prepared for Bumps and Bruises

As the parent of a small child, you'll be administering a lot of first aid—particularly once your child is getting around on her own. You can minimize hazards by childproofing, but your baby will still get her fair share of "owies" in her first year.

You'll need:

- First aid manual
- Telephone number for Poison Control

- Sterile gauze
- Steri-Strips or butterfly bandages
- Soap
- Ipecac syrup
- Activated charcoal
- Adhesive strip bandages (Band-Aids)
- Adhesive tape
- Antiseptic wipes
- Elastic bandage
- Antibiotic ointment such as Bacitracin
- Hydrocortisone cream
- Tweezers
- Calamine lotion
- Cold packs (instant, or keep one in the freezer; use a bag of frozen vegetables in a pinch)
- Cotton balls
- Scissors

80. Treat a First-Degree Burn

Soak the burned area in cool water for at least twenty minutes or until the pain fades. You can hold the burn under cold running water or put ice and cold water in a bowl. Don't use ice alone; it can increase the damage to the skin. Do not put butter or other greases on a burn—they'll trap the heat and make it worse. And don't pop any blisters that develop; just cover them with a bandage. Redness and a slight swelling are signs of a first-degree burn (the least serious); blistering and significant swelling indicate a second-degree burn; areas that seem white or charred indicate a third-degree burn. If you suspect a second- or third-degree burn, see a doctor immediately.

81. Keep Poison Control on Speed-Dial

If your baby ingests something poisonous, take away the poisonous substance, and remove any left in your baby's mouth with
your fingers. Keep anything that you remove for later analysis.
Check for severe throat irritation, drooling, breathing problems,
sleepiness, or convulsions. If you see any of these symptoms, call
an ambulance. If not, call your local poison control center. They
may tell you to induce vomiting by administering ipecac. Do
not give your baby ipecac without checking with poison control;
some poisons can do more damage when vomiting is induced.
Or you may be told to neutralize the poison with a glass of milk
or activated charcoal.

82. Soothe a Sunburn

Give your baby a bath in cool water or soak some washcloths in
water and lay them over the burned area. After he's dry, spread
aloe (100 percent) on the burned area.

Or soak your baby in a lukewarm bath with either a quarter
cup of baking soda or a cup of comfrey tea (comfrey reduces
swelling). If your doctor has given you permission, you can give
him some ibuprofen or aspirin (if there are no fever or cold
symptoms).

If the sunburn blisters, if your baby gets a fever or chills, or if
he seems very sick, call the doctor.

83. See a Doctor for "Smiling" Cuts

Stop the bleeding by applying pressure directly to the cut. If
the cut "smiles" (the edges gap apart farther in the middle than
on the ends), is deep, or may have dirt or glass stuck inside,
see a doctor. Wash it thoroughly with soap and water, apply an

antibiotic ointment, and put on a Band-Aid. If the cut isn't particularly deep or long, it will probably stay closed on its own. Or you can bring the edges together and fasten with a butterfly bandage or Steri-Strip before covering it with a regular Band-Aid.

84. Avoid the Heimlich for Choking

If your baby's choking, first give him a chance to cough and clear his throat himself. If he can't breathe, dial 911 then place him face down on your arm or lap so that his head is lower than his torso. Support his head and neck. Using the heel of your hand, give five quick thrusts between the shoulder blades. If he's still not breathing, lay him on the floor on his back and, using two fingers, press quickly along the breastbone five times. Keep repeating these two moves. Do not use the Heimlich maneuver; a baby's bones and organs are too fragile.

Part 4

Choosing a Pediatrician and Knowing When to Call

Before you became pregnant, you probably only saw a doctor once a year for your annual checkup. But now that you're expecting a baby, it's time to get used to the idea of seeing many more medical professionals on a regular basis, since there will most likely be monthly visits to monitor growth and assess needs. That's why it's very important to choose a medical team with which you feel comfortable. At your childbirth class, you'll learn how to make the best choice for you and your baby.

85. Choosing a Pediatrician: Ask for Recommendations

From birth to around age eighteen or even twenty-one, your child will be seeing a doctor on a regular basis, and preferably someone you've spent a lot of time in choosing. A professional you feel comfortable discussing your developing child with is tantamount to a having a healthy child.

The first step in finding a good pediatrician is to talk with other parents, your obstetrician, or your regular family doctor. You should then look in your insurance directory to make sure that the recommended physician is covered by your plan.

86. Get More Information

Once you have a preliminary list of pediatricians to choose from, you should call the pediatrician's office to listen for a friendly voice. If his or her staff seems rushed, or impatient, or just plain rude, hang up and call the next one on your list. Medical professionals should realize that they are representatives of the physician and practice; therefore, they should always be kind and patient with anyone on the other end of the phone—no matter who or when.

87. Set Up an Interview

When you get a positive feeling from a receptionist or nurse's aide, you should set up an appointment to interview the pediatrician. Most will not charge you for this time with them; it should be considered a sales call, since you are in effect interviewing them for the job of caring for your little one; it is not a job you would entrust to just any doctor on the list.

88. Ask Questions!

Once you have an appointment scheduled, jot down some questions you might like answered by the pediatrician. Ask the doctor about his or her general approach to working with children. Questions such as, "What do you find most fulfilling about working with youngsters?" will net you some telling answers. If the doctor says, "I most enjoy helping kids to grow, learn, and adjust to their world," you've got a good one. If, on the other hand, the response is that it was either this or become a veterinarian, continue on your search.

89. Inform Your Chosen Pediatrician

Once you've chosen your pediatrician, it might be a nice gesture for you to let the doctor know why he was chosen. If it's the doctor's responsiveness that impresses you, say so. If it's the calm, quiet atmosphere you like, mention that, too. Be sure to be as specific as you can. Communicating clearly about the traits you're happy to have found in a pediatrician will help the doctor keep up the good work.

90. Know What to Expect

The first visit with the pediatrician usually occurs at the hospital within hours of birth. During this visit, the doctor will examine

mommy info

Though you may feel silly panting and blowing with a pillow up your shirt and a roomful of other couples doing the same, these types of exercises can actually help alleviate your delivery-room fears well in advance—not to mention give you and your partner something to joke about on the way to the hospital.

55

the baby from head to toe, making sure that all of the baby's vital signs are stable and consistent with those of other newborns. The doctor will then report all of her findings to you in your hospital room; you will begin hearing about "percentiles" (benchmarks against other typical newborns) and how your baby measures up against others his age.

Within three to five days after delivery, you will return to the pediatrician's office for another checkup. All of the vitals will be checked again, including your baby's weight and an exam for jaundice, and you will also have the chance to discuss any feeding, sleeping, or related problems with your pediatrician.

91.   Schedule Well-Baby Checkups

"Well-baby" visits need to be scheduled at one, two, four, six, nine, twelve, fifteen, eighteen, and twenty-four months, and here the doctor will cover everything from a brief physical to a discussion of baby's particular growth stage to track his physical, emotional, and motor development. You will constantly be talking about baby's eating habits. After two years of age, your child will need only an annual checkup.

92.   Become Familiar with the Vaccination Schedule

Immunizations should occur at two, four, six, twelve, fifteen, eighteen, and twenty-four months. These immunizations protect against the following diseases:

- diphtheria
- pertussis (whooping cough)
- mumps
- measles

- tetanus
- rubella
- hepatitis A and B
- prevnar
- chicken pox
- rotavirus
- haemophilus influenzae type B

93. Know What to Expect: Hepatitis B and *Polio* Vaccines

The Hepatitis B vaccine, which helps protect infants at risk of developing the disease from infection passed by the mother, is often given to babies first at birth and then at two and six months. Some babies, albeit a small percentage, develop minor, temporary side effects such as a rash. This is nothing to worry about and will go away on its own within a few days.

Your baby will also need to have the inactive polio virus immunization, and this vaccine is given at two, four, and eighteen months. Babies used to get the active virus version, but since there was a 1 in 750,000 chance of contracting the disease with the first dose, many physicians felt that was too risky. In concordance with these fears, the Centers for Disease Control and Prevention (CDC) made a new recommendation for U.S.

mommy info

Perhaps the best news of all is that there are now combination shots for some immunizations. These shots eliminate the need for three injections at one time—something that all babies (and some weak-stomached parents) will definitely appreciate.

polio immunization, so the enhanced inactivated polio vaccine (eIPV) is now the only option.

94. Watch for Symptoms after MMR

MMR is the measles, mumps, and rubella vaccine, which baby doesn't get until he is fifteen months old, when the immune system is even stronger. Up to 15 percent of babies show adverse reactions, not immediately after the shot but within two weeks of immunization. Symptoms such as rash, fever, or swollen lymph glands could indicate a reaction; and it is best to notify your pediatrician immediately if you notice such reactions.

95. Build a Relationship with Your Pediatrician

Once you've established a partnership with your pediatrician, how can you keep the relationship a positive and productive one? First, you should follow the rules and policies of your pediatrician. Keep the doctor's information sheet handy, and refer to it often. Parents who expect special treatment will ultimately turn off a pediatrician and damage their working relationship. Also, to save the doctor time, come in with as much information as you can muster. Things like temperature, symptoms, and general behavior of the baby will provide some clues to baby's illness.

96. Listen and Wait

Be willing to try what the doctor says. If she doesn't feel that a medication will nip the problem or that the illness must simply run its course, don't argue, but do ask questions if you are not convinced. If, on the other hand, you try leaving baby to fight off the problem and the symptoms get worse, do call the doctor back to try another approach.

If you can wait until morning, do so before calling the doctor. Leave the nighttime and weekend calls for emergencies only. This is a hard concept for first-time parents, to whom anything unusual may seem like an emergency.

97. Think Before You Call

First-time parents tend to worry about their baby more than veteran parents do, mainly because every new noise or cry makes them worry about illness. But it's important to remember that your baby operates much like you do. There can be occasional bouts of diarrhea, some gas or tooth pain, and even crying for no real reason. Your baby might even have a constipated moment or two. None of these problems is necessarily an indication of serious illness, so you need not worry if they happen occasionally or seem short lived. Fortunately, most pediatricians' offices have nurses on staff to field calls from worried parents.

98. Know When You Must Call

Here are some times when a call to the nurse at your pediatrician's office is absolutely necessary:

mommy info

Don't use your baby's appointment as an opportunity for all your other children to be seen by the doctor. Pediatricians agree that this one-stop-shopping approach not only takes too much of their time (affecting other scheduled appointments) but also is unfair to them. If others in your family need to be seen by the doctor, schedule a separate appointment for each.

- When baby's temperature is higher than 101 degrees (rectally), or above 100.4 degrees if the infant is less than three months old.
- When baby sleeps long or doesn't wake easily.
- When baby is unusually fussy or irritable.
- When baby refuses to feed well or eats only a small amount before crying in a high-pitched manner.
- When baby isn't wetting at least one diaper every four hours or so (for a total of six to eight per day).
- When baby vomits excessively at more than two consecutive feedings, or vomits green bile (if this occurs, call doctor immediately).
- When baby has labored, distressed, or rapid breathing.
- If baby's color tone changes (look for blueness in the lips or fingernails or yellowish skin or eyes).

99. Don't Fret about Minor Skin Irritations

Rashes and skin irritations are common problems among very young babies; everything from laundry detergent to your perfume can cause red, flaky, and itchy skin for baby. The most common culprit, however, is spillage of milk into the folds of the neck. Be sure to keep a bib on baby, and wipe the area after feeding time. Also, use a good baby cream in the affected areas two or three times per day. Eczema, or atopic dermatitis, can occur when infants have rough, red, itchy skin and often improves with moisturizers and a topical steroid cream. Call the doctor if you suspect your baby has eczema.

100. Keep Skin—and Air—Moisturized

When your baby has eczema or other skin conditions, use lots of baby cream and keep baby's nails trimmed to avoid excessive scratching. Use a cool-mist humidifier to keep baby's environment moist. Avoid overdressing baby, and stay away from scratchy materials. Soft cotton outfits that leave baby's neck open to the air are preferable. Take note of any foods that seem to trigger a rash, and eliminate them from baby's diet. Call the doctor if the rash seems to be getting worse or if it doesn't seem to go away.

101. Treat a Slight Fever

The scariest thing a new parent will face is baby's first real fever. (Note: For infants under three months old, a fever is anything above 100.4 degrees.) If baby has a slight temperature, you may be able to bring it down with over-the-counter baby pain reliever. Some fevers are caused by teething pain or perhaps are a reaction to an immunization; these can usually be treated with infant pain reliever as well. However, if the fever is 100.4 degrees or more, you will need to call your doctor immediately. If the fever is accompanied by a rash or if it seems to be hanging on for longer than a few days, call the doctor.

mommy info

For newborns and younger infants, always use a rectal thermometer to get the most accurate temperature. You can still use the digital type for back up. Also, do not use products containing aspirin. They have been associated with Reye's syndrome, a brain disorder.

61

102. When Baby Has a Cold, Keep Passages Clear

Babies can develop a fever prior to showing full-fledged cold symptoms, such as a runny or stuffed-up nose, a cough, red or watery eyes, and lack of appetite.

If you think your baby has a cold, you should use a bulb syringe and infant nasal drops to keep nasal passages clear and open. Put a pillow under the baby's mattress to keep his or her head elevated (or use a product called "crib shoes" to elevate the head of the crib); never place baby's head directly on a pillow, because baby can pull it over and suffocate. If baby becomes fussy, has trouble breathing, is not eating well, or seems otherwise unhealthy, call your doctor for advice.

103. Treat an Ear Infection as Soon as Possible

You should treat an ear infection as soon as you can, since they can be quite uncomfortable for baby and can cause delays in language development (because of hearing difficulties). Ear infections are more frequent in babies than in adults because a baby's Eustachian tube is smaller than an adult's, allowing bacteria a quicker route to the middle ear.

Usually a high-pitched cry and tugging of the ear will tell you when your baby has an ear infection. The more you try to lay the baby down to rest, the worse the crying becomes.

mommy info

If your pediatrician has recommended a prescription medication, use it exactly as indicated. Most antibiotics (amoxicillin is the most prescribed) need to be taken until completely gone. Also, be sure to take baby back to the doctor for a followup exam.

Fever is also common. Finally, baby may eat less because it hurts to swallow. Call your doctor for her advice.

104. Watch for Extremes: Diarrhea and Constipation

The primary causes of diarrhea are a viral or bacterial infection or intolerance to a new food. Call the doctor if the diarrhea contains blood or if baby is dehydrated. Signs of dehydration include a significant decrease in wet diapers (low urine output—less than five wet diapers per day); dry mouth; and sometimes weight loss.

If baby is having difficulty in producing stools, try curling the baby's knees up as he is straining; this can help baby use gravity to push the stool out. If there is still a problem, you could try an increase in water or diluted juice. It's common for breastfed babies to only have bowel movements once a week or so, so it's likely not constipation if the baby is feeding well and the bowel movements are soft.

105. Soothe Your Teething Baby

It can take up to two (long) weeks for baby to cut a tooth; imagine how long baby will fuss and cry if left to fend for herself! Gums will be sore, and baby will drool buckets. These are your major symptoms; now that you know what they are, how can you best help baby? Give her some pain reliever (either acetaminophen or ibuprofen if the baby is more than six months old; or you can try some topical pain reliever such as Anbesol). Provide lots of cool teething toys for baby to gnaw on; always keep at least one in the refrigerator. Keep a bib on baby as often as possible, and change it as frequently as it becomes wet. There are also a lot of homeopathic remedies for teething and these can be very effective. Talk to your health professional or natural health advisor to learn more.

Part 5
. . . .

The Big Event: Delivery Day

In the last month of pregnancy, as you await your sweet arrival, it's hard to stay positive about the whole experience. On the one hand, you have those well-meaning people constantly commenting on how "ready" you look (even weeks before you actually are—further prolonging your agony). On the other hand, you have your own feelings of anxiety and concern over everything from whether the baby's room is really ready to trying to imagine a pain you've never felt before (but, no doubt, have been frightened by—thanks to the stories of every other mother you know).

106. Create a Birth Plan for the Big Day

Working together on a written birth plan is a not only a good way to communicate with your doctor about how you would like your birthing experience to be, it can also be a great way for you and your partner to bond over the impending birth itself.

A birth plan lets your family, friends, and medical team know what you would most prefer in the birthing experience. Just remember, it may need to change. Your parents may have simply relied on doctors to tell them what to expect, but recent generations are generally more actively involved.

107. Pass It On!

Once you've finished writing the final version of your plan, don't forget to give it to your practitioner so that it can be included in your file. You might also pack an extra printout in your suitcase for the trip to the hospital, since your doctor may not remember to bring it. If your practitioner isn't available on the day you go into labor, having that extra printout will be a godsend to the delivery expert on call, whom you may not have ever met before the blessed moment arrives.

mommy info

To make your birthing experience a little bit more comfortable, bring some soft music on a portable CD player (or several CDs that you like, since it might take a while), a picture of a pleasant scene to focus on during labor and a special toy or meaningful item from one of your other children.

108. Be Specific

Be as specific as possible when writing your birth plan. Here are some things you need to include:

- The method you've chosen for delivery (Lamaze, Bradley, Hypnobirthing, Grantly Dick-Read, or the LeBoyer Method)
- A section about where you intend to give birth (at home, in the hospital, or at a birthing center)
- Your plan for how you'd like to manage pain and monitoring of you and your baby
- Thoughts about the atmosphere you'd most appreciate (i.e., warm lights, soft music, or even a water birth)
- Who should be in attendance, and why you want them there (include a call list and try to limit the number of participants); note that insurance regulations or hospital rules may limit participants
- Whether you'll allow any relatives to videotape or photograph the experience
- How soon you'd like to hold the baby after giving birth
- How you'd prefer to have emergency information presented to you

mommy info

Some experts suggest that you try getting on your hands and knees, rocking your pelvis while arching your back, to get the baby to move naturally. This does not always work, but it can sure help ease any back pain you might be experiencing.

109. It May Change over Time

While it's great to have a written birth plan early on in your pregnancy, keep in mind that a lot may change over the next several months before baby's arrival. For one thing, you may well decide to change several elements in the plan based on what you've learned from your doctor, a close friend, or at a birthing class. Like any good plan, you'll need to build in some flexibility so that you can easily modify the plan later on without getting yourselves too far off track.

110. Plan Ahead: Start Packing!

One of the best ways to get ready for the big "D" (for delivery) day is to start packing your bags. Take advantage of this quiet time to pack for both you and your baby—as sensibly as possible. Planning ahead will ensure you have easy access to all of the practical and comfort items you'll want to have on hand at the hospital, including a list of everyone you want to call to announce the wonderful news!

111. Pack Practical Items

You'll need a robe and a nightgown, unless you like wearing the standard hospital issue. If you're going to breastfeed, choose a gown that opens easily in the front. Next, some warm, nonskid slippers would be nice, though the hospital typically has nonskid socks. Hospital floors can be slippery, and you'll be walking to the nursery at least once during your stay. You'll also want to pack a good nursing bra, as well as some nursing pads, in case your milk comes in sooner than you expect. If you're not going to breastfeed, bring a bra that's slightly smaller than you would normally wear to help your breasts return to their prepregnant state.

112. Include Comfort Items and Toiletries

Nonperishable snacks for your birthing coach are always a great thing to pack. Your baby's father is bound to get hungry, especially during a long labor, and you don't want him having to spend time waiting in line at the hospital cafeteria when he could be rubbing your back instead! For easy backrubs, pack a tennis ball or back massager. These items will help him provide extra pressure—a godsend if you have back pain. Finally, pack some toiletries, including your toothbrush, toothpaste, hair brush, makeup, deodorant, and a box of large maxi pads with wings, as you'll need them after the birth.

113. Don't Forget Something to Wear Home!

You'll need one outfit to come home in after the delivery; make sure it's loose enough to accommodate your body comfortably, as you will not lose incredible amounts of weight immediately upon delivery. Include a few pairs of maternity panties and several pairs of socks—you'll need them for the delivery and afterward.

mommy info

If you're feeling a little anxious about the details of the birth, it might help you to learn as much as you can about the stages of labor. If you're like most women, you've already flipped to this section before reading any of the early pregnancy information—to mentally prepare yourself for the moment you've likely dreamed about for quite some time.

114.   Pack for Your Baby, Too!

Since the normal tendency is to overpack, you'll want to prepare baby's travel bag a few weeks before your due date. The easiest way to pack mindfully is to lay out all of the items you think your baby will need on your bed, and take a good, hard look at how much you're packing. Are there items that seem extra or unnecessary? If you really want to be sure, invite a friend over to take a look, then toss aside any items beyond the bare minimum: clothes, diapers, and nail scissors.

115.   Bring Weather-Appropriate Outfits for Baby

Pack at least two gowns that are open at the bottom or that have a pull string, as well as one going-home outfit for baby. Decide what you want to dress the baby in for his first pictures, since Dad will probably take several shots of you leaving the hospital. Bring a light or heavy blanket, depending on the climate or the time of year. Finally, if it's winter and you live in a cold climate, pack a snowsuit. The hospital may give you a cap for baby, but pack one anyway because your newborn's head needs to be covered when you walk out the door, no matter what season it is.

mommy info

Take the time to discuss your feelings and fears with your doctor well in advance of the possible surgery. It might be a good idea to ask the doctor exactly how the determination for a C-section is made so that you are prepared for that option and not surprised if surgery is mandated.

116. Be Prepared for a Change in Position

A breech baby is simply a baby who is presenting its feet first—instead of its head—toward the birth canal. Today, almost all breech babies are delivered via C-section. If your baby is in a breech position before birth, you have a few options. You could see a specialist who can turn the baby or you could try an alternative method such as acupressure. Whichever method you decide to try, do consult your doctor first. Remember, the baby can still turn at the last minute—even during labor!

117. Be Aware before You See a Specialist

A specialist can turn your baby using external manipulation and use of ultrasound to check baby's position. However, some doctors insist that a breech baby is in that position because it is most comfortable—that the baby, in fact, knows, for example, that it has a cord around its neck and that moving makes it tighter. They are growing increasingly skeptical about this procedure, since a few infants have been lost because the umbilical cord was wrapped around the neck at the time of inversion—with the specialist completely unaware.

118. Get Ready for the Stages of Labor

Labor itself takes three stages to accomplish its mission: early labor (about five to eight hours, but possibly longer if this is your first baby), which brings with it irregular contractions that open your cervix to about four centimeters; active labor (about two or three hours), which brings intensifying contractions that are closer together and open your cervix to about eight centimeters; and transition (thirty minutes to two hours), which is hard labor and opens your cervix to the ten centimeters needed for pushing. These are the three parts of Stage One, you will learn more about Stage Two and Three—the birth of the baby and the delivery of the placenta—as you keep reading.

119. Distinguish False Labor from *Real*

Just because there are a few labor pains happening doesn't necessarily mean you're in active labor. False labor is sporadic and unpredictable, and it may disappear altogether if you change position or get up and move around. Real (or active) labor is marked by pain occurring in regular intervals, increasing in intensity until it becomes difficult to breathe or talk through contractions. In active labor, the breaking of the bag of waters can also be a telltale sign that labor is real. Often, a small amount of blood-tinged mucous may pass from the vagina prior to your water breaking—sometimes, your water won't break until the doctor makes it happen in the delivery room! Rely on timing and intensity of contractions as an indicator of labor.

120. *Get Comfortable for Stage Two*

This is the stage where you get to push the baby out of your body and into the world. At this point, if you feel like it, you can try whatever position makes you feel most comfortable (sitting up, lying down, squatting, or a side position). As the baby

mommy info

What's the difference between a doula and a midwife, you wonder? A doula is more like a coach, someone who provides emotional and physical assistance to a couple during the birthing process. A midwife has actual hands-on medical responsibility for everything from prenatal exams to delivery.

moves further down in the birth canal, you will feel more and more like pushing. If your doctor says it's okay, do so.

121. Listen to Your Doctor

If your doctor asks you to pant or blow instead of pushing during stage two, do as you are instructed, since you might have to have an episiotomy if the doctor thinks you might tear your vaginal opening. This will only take a minute to do and most doctors will perform it only if it is necessary (though you should discuss this ahead of time). Stitching you back together after episiotomy generally takes another thirty to forty-five minutes.

122. Consider a Water Birth

According to the National Women's Health Information Center, more women in the United States are using water to find comfort during labor and delivery. In water birthing, laboring women get into a tub of water that is between 90 and 100 degrees. Some women get out of the tub to give birth. Others remain in the water for delivery.

The water helps you keep warm and relaxed. This eases the pain of labor and delivery for many women. Plus, it's easier for laboring women to move and find comfortable positions in the water. Ask your doctor or midwife if you are a good candidate

mommy info

Water birthing is relatively new in this country, so there's very little research on its benefits. Even so, some women say giving birth in the water is faster and easier. Plus, women may tear less severely and need fewer episiotomies in the water.

for water birthing. Water birth is not safe for women or babies who have health issues.

123. Relax for Stage Three

This is the stage where your hormones trigger delivery of the placenta, and it is either pushed out by you or removed by your doctor. The doctor will then check it over for signs of any problems and assist you in the beginning of your recovery by suturing any tears or incisions from an episiotomy. He will likely give you some bonding time with your baby and then visit you later with aftercare instructions and tips.

124. Don't Panic: You'll Hold Your Baby Soon!

Using a rating scale called the Apgar (after Dr. Virginia Apgar, who devised the method of testing newborns back in the 1950s), a neonatal nurse evaluates the baby to determine its health immediately after birth; she then repeats the test one or two more times in the five to ten minutes following birth. This is standard procedure and nothing to be alarmed about; you should ask your doctor in advance of the birth how soon you'll be able to hold the baby; that way it won't be a disappointment to you if this is a moment you've envisioned for some time.

125. Watch for Post-Delivery Trouble

Immediately after the baby is born, you will need to watch for the following signs and call your doctor immediately if you experience any:

- Discharge from your vagina that is heavier than normal, is bright red, or is foul-smelling.

- Fever or sudden rise in temperature.
- Burning on urination or difficulty in doing so.
- Soreness or irritation in your legs or in your breasts.
- Any adjustment problems that interfere with care of the baby.

126. Consider a Doula or Midwife

If you live far away from relatives and want to have the kind of nurturing care that your own mother might provide, working with a doula can be a wonderfully reassuring experience. A doula will stay with you from the moment you go into labor through the birth, and will sometimes even serve as a lactation consultant. If it's a long labor, a doula might give your baby's father a rest and hold your hand through some contractions.

If you prefer a nonsurgical, homelike atmosphere, you can always opt for a midwife-assisted birth plan. This often, but not always, means giving birth at home.

127. Determine Whether an At-Home Birth Is for You

At-home births (usually performed by midwives) are permitted if there are no signs of imminent danger to the mother and the baby seems to be progressing normally.

At-home births differ from hospital births in that you are free to include whomever you'd like in the process. If you'd like your whole family over to have a "welcoming" party for the baby, this option is more available to you than it would be in a hospital birth. Of course, as with any birth, you should prepare for the possibility of an emergency. Should any complications arise, your midwife will call 911.

128. Be *Ready* for an Induced Labor

When a baby is more than a week beyond its due date, a physician may make the suggestion to you that the baby be induced. When a baby is induced, the first step is often placing a prostaglandin gel on the mother's cervix to encourage dilatation. Some women spontaneously go into labor with the gel alone, while others require further medication in order to get things rolling.

129. *Prepare* for *Pitocin*

If you should need more medication, Pitocin is usually the drug of choice. It is given through an IV, and it usually spurs labor on within a few hours. On the downside, many women say that Pitocin causes fast and furious labor pains. The pains are generally more intense and closer together than in a natural labor, but the benefit is that the labor is also generally shorter with induction. Most Pitocin-induced labors are over within a few hours.

130. Forceps Deliveries Are Less *Common*

When labor seems difficult or extremely prolonged, and the natural force of your body doesn't seem to be enough to nudge baby out of the birth canal, some doctors will use forceps to deliver your baby. Forceps are two metal blades built to fit gently onto baby's head; the doctor applies some pressure to draw the baby out. Forceps deliveries are not as common as they were in the last few decades, primarily because some babies have been hurt in the process.

131. Get to Know the C-Section Basics—Just in Case

If your baby is really late, too large, or not well positioned—or when the lives of either the baby or the mother are in jeopardy—a Cesarean section may be performed. If your doctor chooses to perform a C-section (as it's more commonly called), you'll be given a spinal, or epidural, an anesthetic that numbs you and allows you to be awake for the surgery. A tent is placed over your abdominal area, and your partner is usually near your head. Afterward, the placenta is removed and examined, and the doctor will usually perform a check of your abdominal cavity. Once that's accomplished, you'll be stitched up and taken into the recovery room.

132. Ask Questions about C-Sections

If your doctor should decide to perform a C-section, ask as many questions about it as you feel a need to; then try to put it all in perspective. If you had your heart set on a vaginal delivery, don't let the prospect of a C-section ruin your birthing experience. You are still a mother giving birth to her child, regardless of the way it actually happens. And the best thing you can do is put the needs of your child first, which is exactly what a C-section is about, since it is performed as a safety measure for the baby.

mommy info

If you have already planned on a completely natural, unmedicated birth (and your physician has given the okay), you still need to learn about Cesarean births, because there is no guarantee that you won't have one should an emergency arise.

133. Take It Slowly During C-Section Recovery

When recovering from a C-section, you will be encouraged to turn and move around while still in the recovery room so that your muscles don't get cramped. You should make sure that you raise the head of your hospital bed before attempting to turn your body; then place a pillow over your abdomen to keep from popping stitches when attempting to sit up. Try to move into a sitting position carefully, stretching your legs to the floor as far as you comfortably can. Then, with some help from your partner, try to stand for a few minutes. Alert your doctor to any discomfort beyond that which is expected after a C-section.

134. Don't Rush Postpartum Recovery

Physically, you may be feeling extremely tired from the birth experience itself, and your body will need at least four to six weeks to recuperate. Giving birth is something akin to the decathlon. Your body uses muscles you didn't even know you had to accomplish a monumental feat: bringing a new life into the world. Don't underestimate the fact that your body will take its own time to get back to normal after the birth. If you try to rush your recovery, your body could respond with negative side effects and complications, thus extending the recovery period.

mommy info

A severe form of postpartum depression is postpartum psychosis, which affects a very small percentage of the population but has symptoms of wishing to harm yourself or the baby. These thoughts are serious enough to warrant immediate attention (and intervention). Call for help if you experience such thoughts; with professional help, it is absolutely possible to overcome this disorder!

135. Give Yourself Emotional Leeway

Expect your emotions to run the gamut from euphoria to depression. There are plenty of ways you can deal with any stress you might be feeling. First, write down your concerns or worries and share them with someone close. Try varying your daily routine.

If that doesn't seem to work, get a babysitter for a few hours and just do something for you: a massage, a facial, shopping, or even lunch alone at your favorite restaurant. Or take a warm bath and cuddle up in bed with a good book. In those first few weeks home, go easy on yourself—and always make time for you.

136. Don't Be Afraid to Call for Help

If the stress is too much or becomes more severe (leading to depression), seek professional assistance. You should call your doctor if you experience any of the following:

- Inability to motivate yourself to do much except meet the baby's primary needs
- Periods of moodiness or irritability that lead to further depression
- Anxiety
- Insomnia
- Difficulty concentrating or making decisions
- Crying jags or periods of sadness that do not go away easily

All of these symptoms are signs of postpartum depression (PPD), a condition that affects about 10 to 15 percent of new moms (although that number could be considerably higher, since many are afraid to tell anyone what they're experiencing).

137. Distinguish Between *PP*D and "Baby Blues"

Postpartum depression is different from the more common (and shorter-lasting) "baby blues," which typically occur within days of the birth and last a maximum of two weeks. With PPD, a new mother experiences depression that cannot be alleviated without the use of antidepressants, or therapy, or, in some cases, both. Risk factors for PPD include problems with your marriage, depression or anxiety during the pregnancy (or a stressful event), lack of support from your partner or significant others, a history of premenstrual syndrome, or a previous case of PPD.

138. You Won't Be the *Only One* Who's *Overwhelmed!*

Your partner may be feeling the stress of some of this new responsibility, too, and may be as overwhelmed as you are. Don't be afraid to share your feelings openly with each other; you will both need each other's support during this time in your lives.

Above all else, don't be too hard on yourself, particularly if this is your first time being a mother. If you have a hard time dealing with parenting issues, seek the help of a support group for new parents or check out an online support group. There is help out there; you're not alone in feeling overwhelmed.

mommy info

It might take awhile for you and baby to get used to each other's cues. For instance, baby may cry incessantly for an hour or so before you can figure out exactly what's wrong; expect that this might happen, try not to get frustrated, and allow yourself a little time to learn baby's way of communicating.

139. *Get Used* to a New Life!

After nine months together, you and your baby are now embarking on separate, unique lives. And even though you had a life before baby's conception, the one you have now entered into is entirely different.

Before baby's birth, you were your own person. During your pregnancy, you were the mother-to-be. Now, you are baby's mommy. If you want to have a separate identity outside of your child, you'll need to decide how and where it will be.

Whatever you decide, know that your life will be much richer and much fuller than you ever dreamed possible—full of more possibilities, especially now that you and baby are finally two separate entities!

Part 6

Caring For Your New Little One

Once you've had your baby, the thing you'll be most concerned with is how to properly care for her. Remember that the overall health and well-being—including nutrition and exercise—of both you and your baby are your top priorities. It doesn't matter which methods you choose, as long as you choose what's right for both of you. But remember, your postpregnancy routine should be focused on gradual change and development rather than on immediate results.

140. Get the Facts: Breast versus Bottle

You've probably heard from both sides on the issue of breastfeeding. Some mothers (and some doctors) will tell you that breastfeeding is the only way to make sure that baby is getting proper nutrition. Others will say that formula feedings now have better nutrients than they used to contain. Both of these arguments are actually correct. Formula is better than it has ever been, and breastmilk provides excellent protection against illnesses. So, what's a new parent to do? All things being equal, it really boils down to your own personal comfort level and core belief system.

141. Breastmilk Is the Perfect Food

Breastfeeding is the most highly recommended form of providing proper nutrition for your baby. Your own milk not only has the right amount of fat and nutrients to help baby grow but also contains compounds that help build baby's immune system. In fact, researchers at the University of Texas Medical Branch in Galveston say that breastfeeding helps protect the roughly 19 percent of babies who would otherwise have been highly susceptible to chronic ear infections due to genetic abnormalities. These protective benefits lasted long past infancy.

mommy info

If you don't feel comfortable with the way you are feeding your baby, your discomfort level will become evident to the baby, and you could wind up with some feeding problems. Make sure you put Mommy first and get comfortable before you start a feeding!

142. Nursing Takes Practice

Nursing your baby should begin immediately upon birth, to give you and baby a chance to get used to this new method of meeting baby's nutritional needs. Remember that up until this point, baby has only fed on your food and prenatal vitamins—and had room service deliver it via the umbilical cord!

Now, baby has to work a little bit harder for her food. So, when you first begin to breastfeed, expect that it may take a few tries before the two of you get the hang of it. Invest in the services of a lactation consultant who can ease your mind by showing you the proper positions for breastfeeding and how to tell if baby has a good latch.

143. Nurse as Often as Possible

You'll want to nurse every time the baby seems hungry. At the hospital, if you are sure you want to nurse exclusively, be sure to point this out clearly to the neonatal nurses. So often, well-meaning nurses offer to feed the baby glucose water or formula so that you can rest. If you don't want this to happen, be clear and direct in your instructions that baby be brought to you every time he seems hungry. The more you nurse, the more milk you will produce. Experts agree that you should try to feed at least eight to twelve times per day.

mommy info

Contrary to popular belief, breastfeeding is not as easy as it looks—at first. What mothers are made to believe comes naturally may often be trial and error until they get used to it; so don't lose your cool until you're absolutely sure there's a problem that will permanently impede your breastfeeding efforts.

144. Don't Worry about the First Few Days

The first few days, you will not see (or feel) a whole lot of milk. However, your pre-milk has plenty of nutrients in it for baby to consume, and baby actually doesn't need much more in the first days. It takes regular stimulation to make more milk. When your milk comes in, you'll know it: Your breasts will swell, and they may even feel like cool water is running through them. Some women report a tingling feeling. Whatever symptom you experience, you'll know it's time for feeding your baby when your breasts are ready.

145. *Good Positioning* Is Everything

Position baby's chin and nose against your breast, and then make sure baby gets the entire nipple in his mouth. If you just let baby attach to the tip of your nipple, you will not have a good latch; and while baby can still get milk, your nipples will feel like they are nearly being pulled off of your body. If you see tiny sores or blood on your nipples, you likely aren't positioning baby correctly, and your nipples are probably starting to abscess.

146. A Little Milk Can Go a Long Way

In the first few days, when you're still in the hospital, your baby should stay with you in your room if there are no complications

mommy info

You should try to nurse for at least ten minutes on each side to encourage milk production in both breasts. You should also drink lots of fluid before, during, and after feeding. You'll need to stay hydrated in order to produce more milk and to keep your own body in a healthy balance.

with the delivery or with your baby's health. Don't expect the baby to wake you up when she is hungry. You will have to wake the baby every one to two hours to feed her. At first you will be feeding your baby colostrum, your first milk, which is thick and yellowish. Even though it looks like only a small amount, this is the only food your baby needs. As long as the baby doesn't lose more than 7 to 10 percent of her birth weight during the first three to five days, she is getting enough to eat.

147. Keep Tabs on Diapers

You can tell your baby is getting enough milk by keeping track of the number of wet and dirty diapers. In the first few days, when your milk is low in volume and high in nutrients, your baby will have only one or two wet diapers a day. After your milk supply has increased, your baby should have five to six wet diapers and three to four dirty diapers every day. Consult your pediatrician if you are concerned about your baby's weight gain.

148. Wake Your Baby for Frequent Feedings

After you and your baby go home from the hospital, your baby still needs to eat about every one to two hours and should need several diaper changes. In the early weeks after birth, you should wake your baby to feed if four hours have passed since the beginning of the feeding. (If you are having a hard time waking

mommy info

Did you know that your baby will tell you when she is full? Cradle your baby's head, but not so closely that baby can't turn away from you when she is finished eating. That's baby's way of telling you she is done.

your baby, you can try undressing her or wiping her face with a cool washcloth.) As your milk comes in after the baby is born, there will be more and more diaper changes. The baby's stools will become runny, yellowish, and may have little white bumpy "seeds."

149. Your Breasts Will *Regulate* Milk Amounts

You can feel confident that your baby is getting enough to eat because your breasts will regulate the amount of milk your baby needs. If your baby needs to eat more, or more often, your breasts will increase the amount of milk they produce.

Other signs that your baby is getting enough milk are:

- Steady weight gain after the first week of age. From birth to three months, typical weight gain is four to eight ounces per week.
- Pale yellow urine, not deep yellow or orange.
- Sleeping well, yet baby is alert and looks healthy when awake.

The more often and effectively a baby nurses, the more milk there will be.

mommy info

At first your breasts contain a kind of milk called colostrum, which is thick and usually yellow or golden in color. Colostrum is gentle to your baby's stomach and helps protect your baby from disease. Your milk supply will increase and the color will change to a bluish-white color during the next few days after your baby's birth.

150. Make It Easier on Yourself

Hospital nurses mean well and are often quite knowledgeable about breastfeeding. Yet, there are still many who don't really know how to help you. Ask for the lactation consultant first; and if your hospital doesn't have one, ask who the best nurse is on staff to help you. Don't take the advice of just anyone passing by unless it's from someone you trust.

Also, once you're home, consider keeping baby in a bassinet next to your bed. That way, you don't have far to go when baby gets hungry in the middle of the night. And breastfeeding babies nearly always will be hungry a few times at night.

151. Protect Your Nipples

To build up nipple durability and keep from getting too tender, try expressing a little bit of breastmilk and rubbing it into your nipples. Let the milk air dry. This offers your nipples natural protection from dry or chapped skin. Another solution is to use lanolin cream on your breasts; it provides a safe, harmless barrier to skin problems. It isn't necessary to use soap on your nipples, and it may remove helpful natural oils that are secreted by the Montgomery glands, which are in the areola. Soap can cause drying and cracking and make the nipple more prone to soreness.

152. Promptly Treat Engorgement

It's normal for your breasts to become larger, heavier, and a little tender when they begin making greater quantities of milk. This normal breast fullness may turn into engorgement. When this happens, you should feed the baby often. To relieve engorgement, you can put warm, wet washcloths on your breasts and take warm baths before breastfeeding. If the engorgement is severe, placing ice packs (or frozen vegetable bags) on the breasts between nursings may help.

153. Look at the Bright Side of Breastfeeding

The benefits of breastfeeding are not limited to your baby. You too can reap some rewards, including weight loss (if you breastfeed for at least three months); a uterus that contracts more quickly (since feeding stimulates contraction); and a lower chance of breast cancer (for you and, believe it or not, for female babies who were breastfed). Also, breastfed babies tend to spit up less than formula-fed babies do. Best of all, it's free and always available, no matter where you are. You can also use a breast pump for times you can't be there to ensure that your baby is getting breastmilk at all times.

154. Choose When to Wean

Although children in some countries continue breastfeeding until they're four or five years old, most American moms prefer to have their children weaned much earlier. Typically, that means weaning baby off the breast starting at six months of age—at the same time more solid foods are being introduced. Make sure to consult your pediatrician and the American Pediatrics Society to determine when the best time to quit breastfeeding is for you. To stop breastfeeding, you may alternate solid and formula

mommy info

If you're on a strict vegetarian diet, you may need to increase your vitamin B12 intake and should talk with your healthcare provider. Infants breastfed by women on this type of diet can show signs of not getting enough vitamin B12.

feedings with breastfeeding until baby gets used to eating more of the newly introduced foods. Some women also begin wearing a bra that is one size smaller than their current size; this creates a binding effect that constricts the amount of milk produced until the milk ducts dry up.

155. Your Decision Is Personal

The decision to feed your baby formula is a personal one; and whether or not others agree, formula is better than ever at mimicking breastmilk in terms of nutrients.

The first discussion about formula feeding should be with your partner. If you both agree this is the way to go, talk with your pediatrician about the appropriate formula for your baby. Many pediatricians suggest using cow's milk formula with iron; however, if your baby has an intolerance to cow's milk, you will need to switch to a soy-based or elemental formula. Neither is a poor choice; it just depends on what baby's specific needs are.

156. Learn the Ins and Outs of Bottle-Feeding

Here are some bottle-feeding tips:

- Sterilize all bottle pieces thoroughly. Use antibacterial soap to clean.

mommy info

Enjoy your bonding time with baby every bit as much as you would if you were breastfeeding. Cuddle, kiss, and love the baby while feeding; share the joy of bonding with baby with others in your family. Let others have a try at feeding baby (with the exception of small siblings who aren't ready to hold baby yet).

- Feed baby every three or four hours the first few months. Follow what your pediatrician tells you about increasing frequency.
- From birth to about four months, feed baby five to six ounces of formula at a feeding.
- Don't heat the formula in the microwave, as this may cause uneven heating and hot spots in the mixture that could burn the baby. Instead, put warm water into a bowl, and then place the bottle inside. Lukewarm is a good temperature.
- Don't reuse formula. Using a bottle over again promotes bacterial growth.
- Stop halfway throughout the feeding and burp the baby. Burp again after baby is finished.
- Keep the bib on for about fifteen minutes after feeding—formula-fed babies often spit up in that time frame, and you'll want to be ready!

157. Watch for Signs of Readiness

When your baby reaches the age of four to six months, or starts showing signs of readiness, such as no longer being satisfied with straight milk at regular feedings, your pediatrician may recommend that you start him on solid foods. That doesn't mean you're suddenly going to serve steak and potatoes, but it does mean that baby is moving on to new (and more challenging) fare. You'll start with rice or oatmeal baby cereal, before moving on to jars of baby food, homemade foods, and finger foods. Finger foods can be started as early as eight to nine months, or once baby has developed a pincer-grasp.

158. Try Out New Foods

Some babies develop food allergies, which is why your doctor will recommend that you try a specific food for at least two to three days in a row before moving on to another new item. This way, if a rash develops, you'll be able to quickly identify the reason behind it. Babies can develop allergies to nuts, egg whites, and strawberries; that's why many pediatricians recommend avoiding foods containing these ingredients. Of course, nuts are very bad foods for babies, since they can be choking hazards; keep them far from the reach of tiny (and curious) hands!

159. Choose Between Cloth and Disposable Diapers

After feeding the baby, the inevitable will happen. You'll have to change a dirty diaper. One of the first choices you'll make as a new parent is which type of diaper to use on your baby. Here you'll need to explore the pros and cons of all options. The "bottom" line is this: You should choose what is most comfortable for the baby and convenient for you.

160. List Pros and Cons: Cloth Diapers

You can purchase a set of fifty or more diapers and wash them for reuse. Your baby may go through six to eight diapers per

mommy info

Some doctors recommend sticking with baby cereal for as long as baby will eat it. Their reasoning is that baby cereal is better tolerated and less likely to cause allergic reactions than other foods. Also, many doctors recommend limiting fruit juice to four to six ounces per day for a baby over the age of six months—diluting it to prevent diarrhea.

day. **Pros:** You can save a lot of money on diapers. **Cons:** It's a lot more work, and you'll go through tons of heavy-duty detergent in the process. Some reports indicate that home washing machines don't sterilize the same way commercial units do. Also, cloth diapers often leak—leading to more wet clothes.

You can hire a service that drops off clean new diapers and removes the dirty ones once per week. **Pros:** It's convenient and environmentally responsible. **Cons:** It's costly and annoying, particularly if you miss your dirty diaper pickup.

161. List *Pros* and *Cons*: Disposable Diapers

You can buy these virtually anywhere, and their manufacturers claim that they are friendlier than ever to the environment. **Pros:** They are convenient and readily available; these diapers are also great for travel. They are also less likely to leak than cloth diapers, and easier to change. **Cons:** They can be expensive, and are not as environmentally friendly.

162. *Get Ready* for Lots of Dirty Diapers

Here are some diapering tips for new parents:

- Take off the dirty diaper, wiping away as much stool as you can with the front of the diaper and using a warm wash cloth or baby wipes for the rest.
- Be aware of the differences between boys and girls, and wipe accordingly. For girls, you should always wipe from front to back (and never in the opposite direction) to prevent any bacteria from getting into the vagina. Even baby girls can get urinary tract or kidney infections, and fecal matter in the vaginal area is a primary cause.

- For baby boys, clean a circumcised penis with warm water and apply a thin layer of petroleum jelly to the tip. For boys who have not been circumcised, wash with a warm cloth and do not retract the foreskin.
- Let the baby "air dry" without a diaper for a few minutes to minimize the chance of diaper rash. Then apply some petroleum jelly or natural diaper ointment to the diaper area to keep baby's skin soft and protect it from irritation.

163. Keep Baby Dry

To deal effectively with diaper rash, you'll need to keep baby's skin dry, and change wet diapers as quickly as possible. Allow the baby's skin to air dry as long as you possibly can, since that will help keep skin from getting irritated. Launder cloth diapers in mild soap and rinse well. Don't use plastic pants. Avoid irritating wipes (especially those containing alcohol) when cleaning baby's bottom. Ointments or creams may help reduce friction and protect baby's skin from irritation; however, powders such as cornstarch or talc should be used cautiously, as they can be inhaled by the infant and may cause lung injury.

164. Make Baby's First Bath a Success

Bathing a newborn can be a challenge, but it can be one of the most fun times you have with your baby. Of course, when you're

mommy info

When changing a diaper, you should first be sure you've put all of the changing table supplies within easy reach. Never leave the baby alone on the changing table, not even if there's a safety belt on it. Babies can roll quickly and fall off the table before you even notice a problem.

reading about it, it will seem easy; but you may find it difficult at first if you're not used to a wet little one trying to squirm out of your arms. Try to keep calm, and have your partner with you (at least the first time) for backup assistance.

Feed your baby at least an hour before the bath, so that baby can relax and go to sleep after a pleasant bathing experience—and so that you can avoid any unpleasant surprises in the diaper region.

165. Start with a Warm Bathroom and a Rubber Ducky

Bathe your baby in a warm bathroom. This will help drain your baby's sinuses, and it will cut down on the chances that she will catch a chill. You might also want to keep all bath supplies within immediate reach, including that rubber ducky you've been saving for your baby's special moment. Put baby's towel on the floor (preferably on top of the soft bathroom rug) so that you have your hands totally on baby as you take baby out of the tub. Wet babies can slip easily, and especially so if you have to let one hand go to reach for the towel.

166. Use the Sponge Bath as an Alternative

To give baby a sponge bath, first fill a bowl or small bucket with lukewarm water. Put a sponge in the water, and add a little baby bath if you want. Place a large bath towel on a flat surface (such as a bed, carpeted floor, or kitchen counter). Put the baby on the towel, folding a part of the towel over the baby to keep the warmth in. Be sure to keep one hand over the baby at all times. Wash the baby's face and the rest of his body. Be gentle, talk to the baby to comfort him, and don't move too quickly. Wipe the baby gently to dry.

167. Don't Forget to Care for Yourself

Getting your body back to its prepregnancy shape can be a challenge. If you're trying to lose some additional pregnancy weight, consult your doctor before you start a diet or exercise plan. If you want to diet and are breastfeeding, wait until your baby is at least two months old. During those first two months, your body needs to recover from childbirth and establish a good milk supply. When you do start to lose weight, try not to lose too much too quickly. Losing about one pound per week has been found to be a safe amount and will not affect your milk supply or the baby's growth.

168. Keep Calories within Reason

If you're breastfeeding, you can safely lose weight by consuming at least 1,800 calories per day with a well-balanced, nutritious diet that includes foods rich in calcium, zinc, magnesium, vitamin B6, and folate. Diets in which you consume less than 1,500 calories per day are not recommended at any point during breastfeeding. This can put you at risk for a nutritional deficiency, lower your energy level, and lower your resistance to illness.

mommy info

For the best (and easiest) program in fitness and convenience, try a walking program. Places to walk are always available, and you can take baby along in a stroller if you need to—so there's no excuse for not doing it!

It's highly recommended that you begin every exercise session with a good warm-up. Stretch your calves, hamstrings, quadriceps, and hip flexors, holding each stretch for about five to ten seconds.

To lose serious weight, you'll need to exercise for a longer period of time (thirty minutes to an hour per day, three or four times per week). And feel free to mix and match—walking, swimming, aerobics, or fitness equipment (such as a Nordic-Track). Join a health club that has a babysitting room for maximum benefit—and the option to work with a personal trainer if you decide you need one.

When you finish exercising, remember to cool down. After exercising is when your muscles most need a stretch, so don't forget this step. Do a few knee lifts or kicks (as high as you can) or march in place to bring your heart rate down after exercising. Then repeat the stretches you did in the warm-up, holding each for ten to fifteen seconds.

To get your prepregnancy abdomen back, lie on the floor with your knees bent; slowly breathe in, expanding your chest and abdomen with each inhale. Pull in your abdomen, spreading out your ribs, then exhale slowly and repeat. On the second rotation, press your lower back against the floor, holding the position for a few seconds before releasing on a slow exhale. Repeat this exercise ten times a few times per day.

Or you can work on getting your back back in shape with these exercises. Sitting on the floor with one knee bent and your foot flat on the floor, rest your clasped hands around your knee and use your back muscles to stretch your entire body toward the ceiling. Keep your abdomen pulled in tightly but your shoulders as loose as you can. Alternate knees and do five repetitions per leg. Both exercises will help your back regain its original prepregnancy strength.

169. Include Your Baby in the Fun!

Make exercise time fun time for your baby, too. Prop your baby up in his car seat while you're working out. It can be a fascinating visual experience for him, and you won't get judged, either! Most of all, don't be too hard on yourself. Just because you can't wear an evening gown the month after you've given birth doesn't mean your life is over. Losing weight and returning your body to its prepregnancy fitness takes perseverance and time. Go easy on yourself—and enjoy the great bonding experience of working out with baby!

Part 7

Getting Your Baby to Sleep

You've heard the horror stories. Like the one where you put the baby to bed softly and without incident. At first, all seems well. But then, out of nowhere, you hear that unmistakable cough, then a sputter, followed by a very loud, "WAAAAAA!" You wonder what could possibly have happened in those first few minutes to make your baby morph from a contented little angel into a holy terror. Now the only question is, what can you do to get this baby back to sleep?

170. The Amount Your Baby Sleeps Will Vary

One of the first questions from just about every new parent is, "How much should my baby sleep?" At first, it may seem like your baby sleeps too much, but then again, there may be times when he doesn't seem to sleep enough (especially when you're trying to get some sleep!). The real answer to this question, however, is that the number of hours your baby sleeps will change a bit over the next several months.

Since babies generally sleep about sixteen out of each twenty-four hours, that means they typically aren't able to sleep more than a few hours at a time. In terms of sleep cycles, then, babies experience about seven asleep/awake cycles, often evenly spaced every day.

171. Don't Be Afraid to Wake Your Baby

Many first-time parents believe (mistakenly) that babies are supposed to sleep all day and night until they are a few months old. This is not true. Babies, especially newborns, do require lots of sleep to grow, but they should only sleep at two- to three-hour intervals during the day. The main reason for waking your baby, if she is sleeping longer than three hours at a stretch, is to make sure the baby is getting proper nourishment. If the baby is not getting enough food at regular times throughout the day, it will only serve to make your nights longer.

mommy info

Sleep cycles change over the first six months of baby's life. By the age of six months, your baby will most likely sleep about eleven hours each night, with a one- to two-hour late-morning and late-afternoon nap. Keeping baby on a routine will go a long way toward developing good sleep habits as baby grows.

172. Teach Your Baby to Sleep

Some parents actually lie down near their baby and pretend to sleep, just to get their baby to fall asleep in a more emotionally secure way. Of course, the downside here is that you could really fall asleep, even before baby does, and if you think that might happen, be sure baby is safe in her crib before putting your head on a pillow. Many experts think it's dangerous for your baby to sleep in your bed!

173. Don't Interfere with Self-Comforting

If your baby prefers thumb sucking as a calming way to drift off to sleep, resist the temptation to pop the thumb out of your baby's mouth. Thumb sucking can be a healthy way for any child under the age of five years old to self-comfort—and self-comforting is something you'll learn to appreciate once you start getting a good night's sleep as a result! While some babies choose their thumbs, others comfort themselves with a pacifier (though they're not adept with it at first) or by rocking themselves to sleep. At least for a few years, whatever gets baby through the night is generally all right—so relax!

mommy info

Don't swaddle baby if the temperature is set high in baby's room. Swaddling babies who sleep in very warm rooms has been associated with sudden infant death syndrome, or SIDS. If you choose to swaddle baby, don't forget to turn the temperature down a few degrees.

103

174. Most of the Time, Baby's Hungry

There are plenty of reasons why some babies don't sleep through the night. The baby could have gas or have teeth coming (temporary reasons, of course!) or just want to be rocked in your arms for comfort. Some babies don't sleep well at night because they are allowed to sleep for long stretches during the day. And some babies are just colicky.

Most of the time, though, your baby is just plain hungry. Offer a bottle or a breast.

175. Do a Diaper Check and Try Rocking

If your baby doesn't seem interested in a bottle or breast, check baby's diaper. Change the diaper as quickly and quietly as you can; making a big fuss over the diaper can actually irritate baby more. You should also try comforting your baby. Gently rock the baby in a rocking chair. Or standing up, rock slowly back and forth, gently patting the baby's back. Maybe there's an extra burp in there that needs help getting out.

176. Use the Swaddling Technique

This technique can be very helpful on a sleepless night, but it's important to note that it's only safe for younger infants and newborns. Swaddle or wrap the baby tightly in a blanket, just

mommy info

How can you know when your baby is dreaming? You can watch for signals, such as a twitching leg or mouth movements. These motor movements indicate that baby's brain is sending these signals to muscles, and brain activity is a positive sign of dream activity.

as the nurses did in the hospital nursery. Place the blanket sideways, with a point at the top. Next, place the baby at the top point, and then tuck one side under the baby's body. Pull up the bottom fold, and then wrap the remaining side over the baby's body. You're not cutting off circulation here, but you are providing that feeling of womblike security for your baby.

Swaddling babies who sleep in very warm rooms has been associated with sudden infant death syndrome, or SIDS. If you choose to swaddle baby, don't forget to turn the temperature down a few degrees.

177. Give the Baby a Pacifier

Like them or not, pacifiers are often temporary solutions to crying problems. Some people may say that pacifiers are more for the mother than the baby, and so what if that's true? At least you've bought yourself a few moments of quiet to collect your thoughts while trying to figure out what's wrong.

178. Be Creative!

Try these creative ways to get your baby to sleep:

- Give baby a warm bath. There's nothing as soothing as a warm tub. Many babies calm down as soon as they hit warm

mommy info

Filling a baby chock-full of formula before going to bed, even if it is laced with infant cereal such as rice, can actually make the situation worse, since the baby's intestines get overloaded with work. Problems with tummy gas or spitting up may result from such overfeeding; so be careful how much you feed baby before bedtime.

water. Add an infant massage, and you'll have yourself one calm baby.

- Do a song and dance. Try singing to your baby, and move around the room as you do so. Babies have short attention spans, and can be easily redirected.
- Take baby out for a spin. Take baby for a walk or a ride in the car. Babies love motion, and the motion of an automobile somehow serves as anesthesia for babies. You'd be surprised to know how many miles are put on a car just for a baby's sake.

179. *Put* Baby to Bed

Like all people, baby can get irritable when tired. Put on the baby's lullaby tape or music box, dim the lights, and then walk out. Older babies over six months can be left to cry for at least ten minutes before you return to the room (unless, of course, you're absolutely convinced there's really something wrong). Some crying before falling asleep is normal for most babies.

180. *Remember*: Atmosphere and *Routine*

There are two basic words to remember when trying to calm your baby into sleeping mode: atmosphere and routine.

For atmosphere, dim the lights, put on soft lullaby-by-the-sea tapes, and rock your baby to sleep. Let your baby feel your

mommy info

There is still controversy over which method really works best. However, most pediatricians discourage new parents from letting a colicky baby cry it out. They reason that a colicky baby is usually less than two to three months old, and that's simply too young to be left alone to cry for long periods of time.

heartbeat; it's calming and comforting to the baby, reminding him or her of that special time in the womb.

Stick to your routine with baby as much as possible. Write it down if you find it hard to remember. Figure out ways to stick with your routine even when you're on the road—stop and feed your baby at the same time you would have at home. Routine helps a baby to feel secure, and a secure baby is a well-adjusted (and relatively quiet) one.

181. Be Prepared for Colic

Colic is a period of crying and fussiness in a baby. Pediatricians sometimes refer to colic as a baby's "daily freak-out," particularly if it occurs around the same time every day. For many parents, this period of fussiness tends to occur in the 7–9 P.M. range.

Why do babies get fussy later in the day? Perhaps because they are at the halfway point in their eating schedule; their little bodies may have had a lot to process thus far and yet have a way to go before resting for the night. Occasionally a baby who has frequent awake times during the day will get cranky by sunset, possibly as a result of overstimulation.

182. Try a Few Approaches

When the baby cries for a prolonged period of time (half an hour) or the cries seem pierced by high-pitched tones, there are still some things you can do to set your mind at ease.

First, try giving the other parent a shot at it. You'd be surprised how much good a small break can do for you as you cope.

Next, take baby's temperature. If your little one has a fever, crying is definitely a way of letting you know. Call your pediatrician for advice (especially if your baby has a fever). There could be teeth coming soon.

When all else fails, call your pediatrician. If your baby just doesn't seem right or isn't responding to any of the suggested methods of calming, your pediatrician may be able to help.

183. Choose to Stay or Go

There are two basic schools of thought on crying babies who won't sleep. The first is to simply let the baby cry itself to sleep, only returning to the crib if something seems seriously wrong. Some parents who have tried this method swear by it, saying that the crying time gets shorter each day until baby can finally go to sleep without crying.

Other parents prefer a more hands-on approach and aren't afraid of spoiling a small baby with on-demand cuddling or comforting. Their point of view is that babies need to know they can depend on their parents when they need them.

184. Learn about Sleep Methods

Widely known as the Ferber method, Dr. Richard Ferber's approach suggests that you put the baby to sleep at night when he is still somewhat awake, so your baby learns to fall asleep without you. Soon after you put baby down in the crib the first night, you need to leave the room. You can go back into the room after five minutes have passed, but just to console baby

mommy info

When giving baby a bath, try slowly dripping water onto baby's tummy, or rubbing baby's feet for a little longer than you normally would. Think of what is appealing to you, and then try it out on baby.

with a tummy pat or stroke of the cheek for a short time. Ferber advises against picking the baby up, as this is a comfort solution that baby could learn to use in place of good sleep habits, or as a stall tactic when he is older.

185. Increase Wait Time with the Ferber Method

When you leave the room a second time, you should wait ten minutes before re-entering the room, and if there's a third time, wait fifteen minutes before returning to comfort baby. With the Ferber method, you increase each wait time by five minutes each night, until baby learns to fall asleep without you. Though it may be difficult to listen to your baby's crying, it's important to remember that this method is safe and that your child will learn that crying to bring you back into the room isn't worth the effort.

186. Don't Discount the "No-Cry Sleep Solution"

For parents who don't want to let their babies cry it out, Elizabeth Pantley's book No-Cry Sleep Solution is a welcome approach. Pantley advises parents to set realistic expectations for baby's sleep routine; for instance, if you have a six-week-old that wakes up two or three times each night to eat, that is considered to be normal. However, for problematic sleep issues, Pantley recommends that you:

- Develop a bedtime routine
- Set an early bedtime
- Follow a more predictable daytime routine that's still a bit flexible
- Have baby take regular naps each day
- Help your baby learn to fall asleep without your help

187. Give Baby a Massage

Giving your baby regular massages will not only stimulate baby's muscle development, it can also generate lots of good bonding experiences for both of you. It also has a long history as a folk remedy for colic. You can even take it a step beyond massage by giving baby her regular, soothing bath, followed by an infant massage with baby cream.

188. Give Your Baby the "Spa Treatment"

Start with baby lying on her back. Put some baby cream in your hands and rub your hands together to create warmth. Rub some cream on baby's face, then neck, and then stomach. Using more cream, repeat the warming process, and then start rubbing baby's shoulders, working your way down the arms. Massage each wrist and hand, working out to the fingertips.

With additional cream, work on your baby's legs. Thighs are particularly good areas to massage a little bit more deeply on a baby, since they are the largest muscles the baby has at this stage.

Then turn baby over to lie on his stomach and begin to massage from shoulder to buttocks. Massage the legs again, and then work on the feet.

mommy info

Doctors do believe there's some correlation between smoking and SIDS. Babies whose mothers smoked during or after pregnancy are at elevated risk of SIDS. So, if you smoke, there's never been a more important reason to quit. Do it for the health of yourself and your baby!

189. Watch for *SIDS*

Sudden infant death syndrome, also known as SIDS or crib death, is the unanticipated death of an otherwise healthy baby under a year old. For some reason, boys and children of younger moms are at higher risk than others; so are bottle-fed and lower-birth-weight babies.

The current thinking about SIDS is that it could be caused by rebreathing carbon dioxide, a birth defect or brain abnormality, or simply problems breathing when baby's on his or her stomach.

190. Know the *Risk* Factors

Since the cause is unknown, remember that risk factors for SIDS include putting a baby to sleep on her stomach or side, allowing baby to get overheated, and exposure to second-hand smoke. Infants and children under the age of two should never be allowed to sleep with pillows; infants should always sleep on firm mattresses and be put to sleep on their backs. The national "Back to Sleep" campaign encourages babies to sleep in this position, as it minimizes opportunities for oxygen depletion.

When baby is old enough to roll over in the crib, he may wish to sleep on the stomach versus the back. However, by this time, the baby will be well past the age of highest risk for SIDS.

Not every case of SIDS can be traced back to smothering. Doctors believe there could be several other factors at play, such as brain stem abnormalities involving imbalances in the way the brain processes the neurotransmitter serotonin. Researchers hope to soon develop a diagnostic test for this brain stem defect.

Keep in mind that doctors do believe there's some correlation between smoking and SIDS. Babies whose mothers smoked during or after pregnancy are at elevated risk of SIDS. So, if you smoke, there's never been a more important reason to quit. Do it for the health of yourself and your baby!

191. Get on a Schedule

The most important thing of all is to get yourself and your baby on a sleeping schedule or routine as soon as possible. Humans have internal clocks that tell them when to sleep, but babies often take fuller advantage of sleep during the day; hence, the saying, "She has her days and nights mixed up."

If sleep is still a challenge, watch how your baby prefers to fall asleep; in the beginning, it was likely to be right after nursing or being bottle-fed. Keep a ten-day record of baby's rhythms, like what time he wakes in the morning, when naptimes seem to occur naturally, and what seems to work best to relax baby at night. If you follow your baby's natural rhythms, you might find that this is the best way to get baby on a sleep schedule that really works—seamlessly and painlessly!

192. Make Sure Everyone's in the Loop

Once you're all on the same page, as well as on a better schedule, discuss your nap routine with your daycare provider to be sure baby isn't getting too much sleep during the daylight hours. Write baby's sleep schedule on a wipe board in your kitchen so that you don't forget. Try to schedule busy activities (such as a trip to the zoo or the library) at peak-awake times versus during restful naptimes.

Remember, try to stick to a schedule of two to three shorter naps during the day for baby, followed by a (hopefully) full night's sleep. If you can manage a daily routine like this with little fluctuation, you'll all be able to reap the benefits of a good night's sleep—every night!

Part 8

Mom, Dad, and Baby: Bonding Time

Your baby is just waking up from a nap, and you tiptoe carefully into the room. You walk up to the crib, look over the rail, and you see a glimmer of a smile from your baby—a gift from baby to you. Is baby as attached to you as you are to him? Yes, but you are each attached for different reasons. Unlike adults, babies do not make attachments based solely on love; they also feel a biological imperative to bond.

193. You're Not Alone

If you're concerned about your ability to bond with your new baby, you should be relieved to know that you are not alone in your fears. Most new parents feel some uneasiness over whether they will be able to form a close family. After all, you've never had to do the work of building a family before; up until this point, you've only had to be a member of one. However, if some time has passed and you still don't feel a real bond with baby, call your obstetrician, since it could be a sign of postpartum depression. Not to worry—help will be on the way if you simply reach out!

194. You'll Learn What Baby Needs

For the first two months, your baby will simply need to have basic needs met; you will bond with baby while feeding, changing, or rocking her. Until the first spontaneous smile is given to you, you won't have tangible evidence of bonding.

After two months, your baby begins to develop a personality, building on patterns established during those first few months. At this stage, you begin to notice patterns. When baby is wet, the cry is even pitched; but when the baby is hungry, the cry may become quite high pitched. Baby is dependent on you at this point to learn his or her signals.

mommy info

Do babies get angry? Yes—but not usually until they are at least six months old. That's because anger is primarily about something that has changed or been taken away, and baby doesn't usually notice such disturbances until he or she is at the six-month mark. The emotions of an infant are, at best, crude attempts to get needs met.

195. Pay Attention to Signals

To decipher baby's distress signals, all you have to do is go down the list of baby's basic needs: Does the diaper need to be changed? Is baby hungry again? Does baby need a nap?

Other emotions are more perplexing. What is baby really smiling about? Babies begin life with little if any muscle control in their faces; thus, the first smiles are actually reflex smiles. After the baby is a few weeks old, the smile becomes more controlled but is still quite random. The best smiles come between four and six months, when baby begins to smile at the puppy, or the toy, or directly at you (returning your smile).

196. You're the Teacher

The things your baby sees, hears, and does help her to learn about the world, and also generate an interest in the people and things in the immediate environment.

Your baby's growing little mind has come into the world like a sponge, ready to absorb all kinds of interesting things. But most important, your baby is learning from you how to be a person. At the same time, you are learning to be a parent, watching your baby for cues that will help you communicate more effectively. Learning to pay attention and respond positively to each other will help you both to bond.

mommy info

Experts say that responding to your baby in a loving and attentive way helps him to learn—so talk to your baby often! Provide your baby with a variety of experiences (talking, singing, playing games) to help baby explore his world safely, positively, and imaginatively.

197. Create Quality Time

Creating special moments that will last a lifetime isn't a difficult thing; all you need to do is be sure to catch baby at the right time. The best time during the first few months for bonding with your baby is right after feeding and changing. At that time, most of baby's needs have been met, and baby will generally be in a happier mood.

If you work outside the home, concentrate on spending quality time with your baby when you return home from work. Quality time is time you set aside for baby—and baby alone.

198. Invite Dad in on the Bonding!

If you're a dad having a hard time thinking of ways to bond with your tiny new bundle of joy, here are a few ideas to start the wheels turning:

- Carry baby with you in a sling or backpack as you tend to chores.
- Go for walks with baby in a stroller, backpack, or sling.
- Take the night shift for bottles and rocking.
- Watch the game together.
- Eat together—and share some food when baby is able to eat solids.
- Take naps together (safely).
- Be the keeper of snacks and goodies (like Cheerios or vegetable slices).
- Help baby learn new things by reading together.

199. Focus on Quality—Not Just Quantity

Many first-time parents, guilt stricken over their time away from baby, try to fit every single activity into a half hour with baby in the early evening. This practice not only is unnecessary (since baby doesn't have a concept of time) but also can lead to overstimulation for the baby; and the parents could misread the baby's irritability as an expression of dissatisfaction with their being away all day.

Give yourself credit for all that you do accomplish with baby, and give baby a break whenever she needs one. Creating a lasting bond depends more on sincerity than on longevity.

200. Talk to Your Baby

When talking to your baby:

- Keep it short and sweet. Use short, simple words like happy, ball, puppy, and kitty when you talk to your baby. Babies can only process a few syllables at a time; so keep it simple.
- Use toys as visual cues. Find a favorite toy; tell baby the name of the toy (bear, rattle, etc.), and use its name frequently.
- Clap baby's hands along when you play word games. Physical activity can help baby associate learning new words with something that feels good.

mommy info

It's hard not to take baby's tears personally when you feel uneasy about your situation, but realize that the baby isn't keeping track of your hours together. All babies know (and need to know) is that there are people in the world who love them, care for them, and spend time with them.

- Narrate everyday activities. When you show baby a diaper and then say the word, baby starts to associate the things she sees with words.

201. Read to Baby

Short, simple books that have touchy-feely features (such as mirrors for baby to look into or fake fur to touch) are a good starting point. Since much of a baby's early processing occurs through sensual, hands-on experiences, books that offer opportunities for baby to have sensory experiences are great. Books of rhymes are good, too, since there is repetition of sounds.

202. Communicate by Sign

Baby sign language is a relatively new concept for parents who want their babies to express their needs in a special, and often more direct, way. Despite its initial challenges, it can be a great way to bond with your child until more language skill is acquired.

If you choose to sign with your baby, start slowly when the baby is at least six months old. Begin with just a few simple concepts like "milk," "sleep," and "eat" before moving on to more descriptive words. Always use the sign with the activity so that baby can connect visual cues to the hand signal for each specific concept.

mommy info

Don't expect too much in the beginning! Make sounds slowly, mouthing and saying "o-o-o" and giving baby ample time to hear (and eventually repeat) it. After about a month of this, baby should finally repeat the sound, and baby's language development skills will be off to a great start.

203. Show Your Love

Your baby begins life with the most important ingredient to development: love. Loving your baby is the first step in building a secure environment, one in which baby can grow and learn and feel your support every step of the way. Take your time with day-to-day activities, such as feeding, rocking, and singing to baby. Set the tone for good habits early.

204. Be Positive

Encourage baby with your vocal intonation. When baby achieves something, enthusiastically say lots of, "Good girl!" The first time baby tries to talk, encourage her with your voice, even though baby's sounds don't make sense yet. Have you ever known a puppy (or a person) who didn't keep trying after being positively encouraged?

Use your baby's name often, and associate it with different things. Say, for example, "Kelsey is a good girl" or "Andrew can talk!" Build language skills early in your child by planting positive pictures in her mind.

205. Set a Warm Example

Every baby has a unique personality—traits that you will discover through lots of great daily interaction. Just remember that,

mommy info

Proponents of baby sign language say that babies who sign can communicate their wants or needs earlier, more frequently, and with less frustration than other babies. Some experts say that signing babies may even be able to learn foreign languages more easily later in life!

at least in the beginning, many of baby's actions are simply mirroring your own antics; that's why it's really important to set a positive tone with baby through fun, yet calm, interaction. Keep stimulating baby's mind, and nourishing baby's psyche with warm, loving thoughts. Do those two things on a daily basis, and you'll find that you do indeed have the best (and most emotionally secure) baby ever!

206. Help Baby Build Confidence

Some babies readily accept new situations, people, toys, or surroundings without so much as batting an eyelash, while others can't seem to move without a crying fit. For slow-to-transition types, move slowly from one activity or place to another, giving baby time to accept that something has changed. Hold baby close, swaddle baby, or sing softly as you gently move from one situation to another. Over time, baby will build confidence and learn to be more secure, making him a much better playmate for other babies in social settings.

207. Know What to Expect from a Playgroup

Picture several parents sitting around in a circle, babies on their laps. As they sing, "The Wheels on the Bus," they clap baby's hands together or bounce their knees in time to the music. After

mommy info

Remember that babies can do no wrong. They aren't capable of distinguishing behaviors, so you cannot punish a baby. Never shake or hit a baby. Be caring and supportive. You will get your chance to teach baby when he or she becomes a toddler and is more capable of processing right and wrong.

the song is over, the babies play "So Big," with parents stretching their arms and legs to show how big they are (and, of course, to exercise them). Someone brings out a xylophone, and babies then get to try their hands at making music.

These babies come from all social, economic, and ethnic groups, and from different backgrounds. The only thing they have in common is their love of play.

208. Join Up!

If you aren't a member of a playgroup, you might do well to consider joining one. Such groups can be a fun way to explore new activities with your baby and with other parents who may offer you interesting (and fun) suggestions. Such groups often use music, art, and educational (yet fun) toys to create new experiences—and as a bonding aid between parent and child.

209. Start Your Own Playgroup

If you can't find a playgroup near you, place a classified ad in your local paper or post flyers at the grocery store or library. There are plenty of good resources to guide you in what games to play and what kinds of toys to have on hand. If you can get enough parents interested, you can ask for a small membership fee to cover expenses such as toys, extra diapers and wipes, snacks, and so forth.

Babies need socialization in the same way that puppies do. Finding a group you and baby feel comfortable with can be a great bonding experience for both of you.

210. Start Learning Those Rhymes!

You'll probably want to learn a few nursery rhymes and games to play with baby. Both have a long-standing history of helping babies to develop. And some stay forever etched in your memories, sending you on a sentimental journey every time you hear them. Even though at first you may feel self-conscious about tugging at baby's toes and playing peek-a-boo over and over again, nursery rhymes and games can be a good way to bond with your child. Playtime can be special time together!

211. Choose Games Based on Development

With myriad choices in the stores today, it's easy to forget that some of the best games for you and baby are the ones where you are playing age-appropriate games together. But where do you start? The easiest way to look at the new games you can create on your own is to match them to specific time frames in baby's development. Much of game-appropriateness is determined by baby's cognitive development.

212. Provide Stimulation

You can learn traditional rhymes and games, or you can purchase state-of-the-art stimulators, such as flash cards that come in black, red, and white (many child-development specialists have

mommy info

Playgroups are especially good for new families living in a place that is far away from family and friends; you can connect with others who experience the same tribulations and joys that you do. It can also be a positive experience for your baby, since babies love to look at and play with other babies.

recommended these contrasting colors for baby's early stimulation and brain development) and feature very simple shapes for baby to stare at. Or try videos featuring the faces of other babies or animated characters, CDs with funny songs for babies, or simple computer games for babies. Mix up the types of stimulation and as with everything else, everything in moderation!

213. Try Out Music Games

If you have an instrument such as a piano or drums, let your baby tap out a few notes occasionally. You don't have to start with formal classes, unless your child appears to be a prodigy. For most of us, it's just a lot of meaningless (yet fun) noise that baby gets to make. It does, however, teach baby a little about cause and effect. If you don't have musical instruments, give baby a pot or pan and a wooden spoon—many babies enjoy these even more than the real thing.

214. TV in Moderation Can Bring You Closer

Experts still disagree on exactly how much television babies should watch—and even whether they should watch at all. Try to be a responsible parent: if baby is watching TV, you should be watching with baby, singing and playing along to make it an interactive experience. Don't use the TV as a babysitter.

Though there are several high-quality shows on cable TV (notably, on Nickelodeon's Nick Jr. and the Disney Channel), many parents still prefer the learning focus of Sesame Street and other public television offerings. Baby will enjoy whatever you enjoy, because you are the one who will make it a fun experience for baby! So clap, sing along, and learn new things together— just keep it age appropriate for baby's developing brain.

215. Bring Your Best Self

The most fun you will have in your playtime with your baby is when you are a barrel of laughs yourself. That's why it's so important that you get the proper amounts of food and rest—you'll want to be in rare form for your adoring little audience. Since playtime can be both a performance and a collaborative effort at times, keeping the rest of your life in balance is pivotal to your success as an entertainer. You have a show to put on, indeed, but the best part is, you'll have full participation from a completely nonjudgmental audience. What could be more fun than that?

216. Deal with Baby's Distress

There are several things that may move your baby out of her comfort zone during the first year—setting off a panic that results in seemingly uncontrollable tears. There are often three major causes of distress in babies: loud noises, separation anxiety, and improper handling.

Loud noises: Approaching your baby quickly and loudly can cause her to cry.

Separation anxiety: Even if the baby knows that the babysitter is sweet, he also knows that you are leaving—and that is a scary thought for a baby. In truth, separation anxiety can be harder on parents than on babies.

Improper handling: Limit contact with small children and pets, at least until you're sure how they will do with your new baby. Slowly integrate them, and always maintain your supervision.

217. Take a Break

When your baby is overstimulated (either by too much noise or overzealous playing), you will know it by her crying. There may even be some rubbing of the eyes, strong kicking, and stiffness when you attempt to comfort her through rocking or holding.

The best thing you can do is put the baby in bed, dim the lights, and put on soft, gentle music. Any other noise or fussing on the part of parents will only serve to annoy your baby further. All babies need some quiet time alone (just as adults do); so respect that need in your baby. Sometimes, fussiness is the only way your baby can tell you that she wants to be alone for a while.

218. *Regular Communication Is Key*

Whether you choose to sign with your baby or communicate with words only, the best way to stay on top of baby's needs is to listen and observe as much as possible. Often, the needs are quite simple and the recommended course of action fast and direct.

Anticipate your baby's most basic needs by keeping food, fresh diapers, and clothing close at hand, and always be ready to share giggles and smiles, since those are a natural part of bonding. Radiate warmth, love, and encouragement, and you will find that you have a baby whose entire world happily revolves around you.

Part 9

Meeting a New World

After you've figured out your baby's feeding and napping preferences, it's finally time to take the show on the road. Introducing your baby to the rest of the world will give you both some well-deserved change of scenery and social time. Once the diaper bag is stocked and the stroller packed, you'll find it isn't so difficult to share all of your previous favorite places, people, and activities with your baby. More than likely, you'll both discover new friends and places on your exciting new social outings.

219. Spread the Joy—Not the Germs

Of course, getting too social too early can be risky, as the more you are around other kids, the more likely that your child will get sick. Even if your child isn't in day care, a few weekly trips to a playgroup and the library might get her a regular cold or ear infection. This might be a good reason to delay getting social until your baby is at least two to three months old (or even older)—especially during cold and flu season.

220. Get Out There!

Zoos, natural history museums, and aquariums offer great escapes—and social opportunities—for cooped-up parents. These options are particularly fun if you have other preschool-aged children. Not only do they offer clean family-oriented bathrooms, good parking, and snack bars, they also offer annual family memberships that cost less than $50 and allow unlimited repeated visits. Your baby will enjoy the movement of fish in aquariums, the low lights, and watching other kids play and run around. You will enjoy the chance to get out and maybe even talk to other parents with new babies.

mommy info

How do I get to the aquarium when I can barely get a shower? Start small! Don't try to spend an entire day out with baby. If you do too much, you'll both be exhausted by day's end and reluctant to go again. Choose the time of day your baby seems most relaxed and happy, or stay close to home.

221. Check Out "Mommy and Me"

If you're at a loss for ideas on what to do with your baby socially, check out "Mommy and Me" (*www.mommyandme.com*), a national playgroup directory and free online resource full of great ideas for activities with little ones. On the site, you can quickly and easily find playgroups, classes, and clubs in your area. Become a member (also free) and gain access to an idea-packed daily activity calendar, or sign up for the e-newsletter and receive tips, product reviews, and more, delivered to your e-mail box on a monthly basis.

222. Go Back to Class

Once you have a better sense of your baby's biorhythms and schedule, you may want to try signing up for a class together. Learn some great new tunes by taking musical classes at Music Together, Musical Munchkins, or Kindermusik. These are great ways to engage with your baby as well as meeting places for other parents. The classes are usually short, sweet, and in a place set up for easy access for parents. They may be in someone's home or at a community center. You may even make some new friends while learning songs and activities you can do with your baby.

223. Search for Mommy Meet-Ups

As you have probably noticed, you aren't the first person in the world to have a baby (although yours is definitely the cutest ever!). There are vast resources for new parents; all you need to do is ask other parents in your neighborhood. Once connected, you'll have many opportunities to socialize, as well as to compare notes when you're having "one of those nights." Maybe you'll just need a referral, or simply want to know which brand of diaper works best—but regardless, all you need to do is reach out for help, and you'll find it's just a phone call or e-mail away.

Mommy meet-ups are a great way to get connected with other parents in your community—or online. To find a meet-up near you, try using a search engine with the keywords "mom," "meet-up," and "[your city name]."

224. Consider a Mother's Club

Mother's Clubs are part of a national organization offering playgroups, lectures, and presentations (usually with babysitting available), outings, and other resources for parents. Offerings vary regionally, but you can check websites and a local phone book or contact your chamber of commerce for information. Those free flyers at the grocery store are also a great source for information on other parenting groups active in your area.

225. Try a Water Babies Class

Since your baby spent nine months swimming around in your abdomen, it's only natural that he would feel comfortable being back in the water. That's why Water Babies classes are so popular—babies generally take to it quickly and easily, as long as you're there for support (both moral and physical).

mommy info

If you strike out with civic groups, check your church bulletin board or other professional organizations to which you may already belong. If you still come up dry, post a bulletin in an alumni or sorority association newsletter offering to start your own playgroup for members.

Through songs, games, and positive word associations, classes emphasize bonding between parent and baby, building communication skills, and getting adjusted to the water. Techniques typically taught for babies in the four- to nine-month range include back floating, submersion, and water safety. Instructors work with parents to help them become comfortable handling their baby in the water—facilitating the deepening bond between parents and their babies.

226. Separation Anxiety—How to Get Through It

While there are plenty of fun things to do with your baby, new parents need time for themselves. Many new parents simply wish for an evening out among other adults; some prefer a quiet dinner alone. But how can you ease the inevitable separation anxiety you or your baby will experience?

First, involve those who will care for the baby "in small doses" before leaving for a longer period of time. Have Grandma come to the house and spend time holding the baby long before you decide to leave; this way, baby and Grandma will be more comfortable with your absence.

227. Leave Comforting Reminders

If you sing to the baby before naptime or bedtime, consider leaving a tape recording of your voice for the caregiver to play

mommy info

Be assertive and ask tough questions before leaving baby with new friends. For instance, do they have guns in the house? Will they follow your schedule for baby? Remember, any deviations from your established routine might be disruptive to your parenting patterns.

133

while you're gone. Or, have your babysitters or caregivers come to the baby's most familiar surrounding (your home) rather than taking baby to their home. The more familiar everything is to your baby, the less stress she will feel. Although you may think they are unaware, babies spend their entire first few months painstakingly taking note of everything in their new world.

If you want, check in with your caregiver frequently—but not too frequently. One or two calls per outing is acceptable, but not a call every hour.

228. Interview Potential Babysitters

Particularly in light of television-show investigations of nannies, au pairs, and babysitters, many parents are leery of letting anyone outside of the family watch or take care of their children for fear of their babies being mistreated by someone they didn't know enough about.

You'll need to interview each candidate, ask for references, and make sure you feel 100 percent comfortable. Start the process as early as your fifth month of pregnancy to give yourself plenty of time to hire the right people.

229. Ask the Right Questions

Ask potential babysitters questions such as: How long have you been babysitting? Do you have references? What do you enjoy most about working with children? What do you enjoy least? Why do you think you would be a good sitter for my child? What would you do in an emergency situation? Is your schedule flexible? Your potential sitter's answers should give you a clear idea whether they're what you're looking for in a caregiver.

230. Write *Up* an Information *Sheet* for Babysitters

When you start making time for yourselves again, you'll need to leave some pertinent information at home for anyone who is babysitting your little one. Here's a list of information you might want to keep on the refrigerator door or near the phone.

- We are out at:
- We will return at:
- A number you can call to reach us is:
- If you can't reach us, call:
- Baby's mealtime is:
- Baby's naptime is:
- For a snack, baby can have:
- Baby is allergic to:
- Baby's bedtime is:
- In case of emergency, call the pediatrician at:
- Police number:
- Fire department number:
- Special instructions:

231. Try a *Parents'* Night *Out* Group

As much as you love your new baby, it'll be a happy day when you realize that you don't have to spend every waking and

mommy info

Be prepared to adjust your expectations—if you were the last one to close down the party before baby, you'll need to prepare yourself that now you'll probably be the first to leave. Get there early and bring all the changes of clothes and bottles you might possibly need to avoid the disappointment of having to leave just because you need something at home.

sleeping moment together. It can be quite a shock to realize that lately, all of your conversations with your partner (or family members) seem to center around feeding schedules, naptimes, and diaper changes. Help is not far away, because every other parent of a newborn is in the same boat. Here, there is empathy in numbers. So, get organized—swap a good night out with other parents and get free babysitting plus the benefit of knowing another parent is watching your precious baby.

Some Parent's Night Out groups are well established and organized with point systems so that one family doesn't end up sitting for everyone else all the time. Others are loosely arranged. If you have older children, they will definitely enjoy a playdate with other kids their age. Pack the pajamas before you send them off so all you have to do is bring them home and put them to bed.

232. Start Your Own Group

Look around your neighborhood and group of friends to see if there are any other parents interested in starting a group or already have one established. Single parents will especially appreciate the break—just make them promise to do something nice for themselves if they don't have a date—and don't let them go home to do laundry! Also, when taking a well-deserved night out, don't forget to leave the name and number of your pedia-

mommy info

Playgroup participants should let others know in advance whether they have any pets, as some participants may be allergic to animals. It's a good idea to have all participants list any pet or food allergies on a form before the first meeting, to avoid any possible allergic reactions.

trician and contact details for where you will be. You may also want to leave the name and number of a relative in the area that might know baby's favorite bedtime song in case you forget to tell them.

233. Get to Know Your Neighbors

Before your baby comes along, it might be a good idea to get to know your neighbors better. Host an ice cream social or just invite your neighbors over for a cookout. Watch how they interact with their own kids, and spend time asking them for parenting advice. Making these kinds of inquiries will give you lots of great insight into their parenting philosophies, and they won't need to know that you are, in fact, screening them as potential babysitters or as friends you'd like to socialize with more after your baby is born.

234. Stay Social

Now that you know you are allowed a social life, don't forget that you can also take your baby with you on various social outings. If you belong to a book group or card-playing group that meets regularly, chances are there are many moms and grandmothers longing for the chance to hold and snuggle a new baby. The holding and snuggling desire may decline rapidly when your baby has a blowout diaper or a colicky crying fit, so you need to be aware of when it is time to leave.

235. Take Your Baby, but Be Considerate

Many young babies sleep soundly in their carriers, so you can tote them to a movie or the concert series you bought tickets for long before your baby got here. Just be aware of others around you;

they also paid a lot for their tickets and may be on a date night away from their own babies, so they won't necessarily want to hear your rendition of "Itsy Bitsy Spider" during a Yo-Yo Ma concert.

236. Seek Out Story Hour

You're never too young—or old—to hear a good story. For another fun (and free) outing in your community, take your baby to story hour at your local library. Many are tailored to audiences with babies and small children, and several feature puppets as well. Your baby will enjoy the sights and sounds, but will also benefit from hearing stories read aloud. Encouraging this kind of social event as early as possible will help foster a love of books and reading later on—so this is definitely an activity worth participating in together!

237. Pack Ahead to Stay Prepared

Pack a diaper bag the night before a big outing, or during baby's naptime. Never raid the diaper bag for diapers at home, or you may get caught diaper-less while you're out and about. Keep special toys (plastic mirrors, rattles, teethers or soft books) that only appear on outings so they will always seem fresh and new.

238. Find a Playgroup

If you have friends with babies the same age, then you have a built-in playgroup. You can chat with your friends while your baby gets to play with "new" toys and experience a different home environment. If you see each other often, then your friend's home will become a "home away from home" as your baby grows, where he will be comfortable with your friends and their different routines. It is a lifesaver to have a place for your child in a pinch when you have an unexpected doctor appointment or trip to the garage with your car.

239. Do a Swap

You might even consider a "toy swap" or "book swap" with friends so babies get to experience new toys that you don't have to buy. Just make sure it isn't someone's favorite before borrowing that squeaky bug toy for a while. When the toys and books return to their original owners, they will be new all over again, if slightly more well-loved. Be a good friend and try to keep toys and books in good condition; wash them, if possible, before returning them. Don't loan out super-favorite irreplaceable toys that came from Grandma's once-in-a-lifetime trip to China; it sets up both you and your friend for an uncomfortable situation if and when they get damaged during what was supposed to be baby's fun time.

240. For Playgroups, Etiquette Is Key

When participating in a playgroup with other parents (and their babies, of course!), having fun is the main objective. You'll want as diverse a group as possible, so that the conversation is always

mommy info

Don't forget to pack sunscreen (at your pediatrician's recommendation) or a hat in summer and winter for baby, as well as all the weather gear appropriate for the season whenever you go out. A bit of planning can make the day so much smoother for you and baby.

interesting. Even though you won't likely hear or see specific signs, babies do pick up on how well their grownups get along and often mimic behavior they see, whether it's for good or ill.

Limit group size to no more than a dozen participants (babies included). That way, the group will be more manageable, and everyone can take a turn as host or playgroup leader. Ideally, the babies should be close in age to better form a peer-based learning environment. Toddlers and older kids can play in another room during playgroup times for babies.

241. Set Ground Rules

It might help your playgroup to develop some "ground rules" or behavioral guidelines for participants. This way, no one will be likely to upset other members with inappropriate comments, "baby boasting" or unfair comparisons. One of the primary reasons people leave groups is that they feel uncomfortable with the comments of other group participants, so head this off at the pass. Here are some good starting points for setting ground rules:

- Set meeting times, dates, and places on at least a quarterly basis.
- Call your host if you're unable to attend or if baby's sick.
- If hosting, clean your house and remove all temptations that could cause safety problems.
- Promptly address your own child's bad behavior—but don't discipline another parent's child.
- Don't change playgroup dates very often, as this will create group instability.
- Always help clean up when playtime is over.

Some playgroups designate two parents to supervise the babies while the other parents have a meeting, complete with an informative speaker on various parenting topics. Consider surveying your group to determine their interest level in having such an arrangement. If half of the members would like to have meetings with speakers and the other half only wants playtime, consider breaking into two groups that rotate their meeting times. This way, you can maximize their interests—and keep membership at worthwhile levels.

242. Give Notice about Pets

One useful ground rule that might get overlooked pertains to allergies. Playgroup participants should let others know in advance whether they have any pets, as some babies participating may be allergic to animals. It's also a good idea to have all participants list any pet or food allergies on a form before the first meeting, to avoid any possible allergic reactions.

243. Look for Family-Friendly Activities

There are so many places catering to families, it's easier than ever before to choose a family outing that everyone can enjoy. With conveniences like family restrooms and breastfeeding rooms, many of the hassles of traveling in a pack are minimized. That's why museums and zoos are such great places for everyone in the family; each family member can appreciate things at his or her own level and pace, and there are plenty of places to take a break if anyone gets tired.

244. Head for the Great Outdoors

Local parks are great, too, particularly if they have hiking and biking trails. Baby can ride snuggly in a bike trailer behind a parent while brother and sister master training wheels, roller blades, or their scooter. Many parks offer free concerts in the summer; that's a great time to spread out a blanket and let baby look up in the trees while listening to music or take a nap while siblings dance and play in the playground. There is also the added advantage of being outside with other families, where no one expects children (or adults) to sit quietly. In settings like these, it's much easier to relax and not worry about noise levels.

And while you're out there, don't forget to pack sunscreen (at your pediatrician's recommendation) or a hat in summer and winter for baby, as well as all the weather gear appropriate for the season whenever you go out. A bit of planning can make the day so much smoother for you and baby.

245. Try the Mall on Rainy Days

The shopping mall beckons again in bad weather, offering rental car- and train-shaped strollers. Some malls even have miniature golf and merry-go-rounds for older kids. Most cities and towns have indoor "play places" geared for the toddler set: a large, open space similar to a great kindergarten classroom, complete with dressup, tricycles, games, and even play structures. Kids can play safely without you having to watch every move like a hawk, so you, your partner, and your baby can enjoy watching the fun.

246. Just Have Fun!

Whether it's at the store, in a special class, or with family or friends, you should relax, have fun, and enjoy your time together with baby. After all, you're making memories together that baby will enjoy hearing about much later on. Enjoy your many explorations of the world, and realize that what's fun for you is often just as fun for baby. If you aren't having fun, neither is baby, but try to laugh it off and do something else another time. When it comes to baby's first social escapades, sometimes false starts and disastrous playdates make the best stories!

Part 10

Day Care and Going Back to Work

For most parents, the choice between staying at home as a full-time parent and returning to work after your baby is born is a difficult one. It's a major decision that can cause inner turmoil. Still, many parents manage to adjust the particulars of their work life so that they can both work and still spend plenty of time with their baby.

Although you may not prefer day care for your baby, the reality is that many families need to rely on the incomes of both parents. Inevitably, this means you will probably need a caregiver for your baby while you're both at work. This could be a friend or relative, or it could be someone you haven't even met yet. Even if you're still pregnant, you want to find a day care that meets all of your expectations—with room on their roster for one more little one.

247. *Remember That You're Good Enough!*

It's easy to get caught up in the belief that despite all the things you do you are simply not good enough. Magazines tell you that working parents don't feel they have enough time with their children and that stay-at-home parents don't feel fulfilled. Somewhere in between is the truth: There is a balance; it just takes a lot of effort to find it.

248. Ask Your Employer

There are several ways your employer should be able to help you balance your work and home life. For instance, perhaps your employer would consider a job-sharing arrangement—one in which you would split a full-time job with another person who can do the same kind of work into two part-time jobs. This way, you and a fellow employee would have more time to spend with

mommy info

Does your company permit use of a flex-time option? If so, your forty-hour workweek could become four days per week at ten hours each—with one extra day off each week. If this sounds like it would be too grueling, ask if you can arrange a workday that begins earlier or ends later than usual.

your families—and the job would still be accomplished for the company without skipping a beat.

249. Find Out if You Can Telecommute

If your job is one that can easily be accomplished at home, ask if you can work from home—and come in only for important meetings, presentations, or the like. Working from home is every bit as challenging for a telecommuter as it is for an entrepreneur, so be sure you're up to it. If you're the type who's distracted by the need to vacuum over the need to finish a report, think twice before considering the telecommuting option. And remember, just because you are at home you will probably still need child care in order to get anything done.

250. Hunt for a Part-Time Job

There may not be much part-time work available in your field, but you might consider branching out into a related field. You just might find work that you enjoy even more than your old job!

Or you could consider a job where you can work evenings while your partner works days (or vice versa). That way, one of you can be with the baby all the time. This option works best when one parent has a part-time job. If that's not possible, make sure to reserve some time each day when you are all together.

251. Figure Out What You Need to Live On

Total up all of your monthly living expenses, and don't forget to prorate those items that you pay for once or twice per year (such as taxes and home or car insurance). Now analyze these expenses against your current and projected new incomes. Can you still meet your monthly obligations if you decide to start a business or stay at home as a full-time parent?

Things like lunches, gas or transportation, and day care add up. Will you still be making any money after these expenses are taken into consideration, or will you simply be paying for time away from your child?

252. Determine Whether a Second Income Is Necessary

What does a second income bring to your family each year? Is it a substantial enough amount that its absence would be harshly felt by all? What would you have to give up in your current lifestyle to stay at home, yet still be comfortable? Downsizing your lifestyle may be an option, since it could help keep you at home with your baby if that's what you most want to do.

253. Live Comfortably with Your Choice

Should you decide you can afford it, staying home is a wonderful option for both parent and baby. It's a beautiful choice that can lead to many terrific memories.

As a final note, remember that these days, it's not always the mommy who stays home with baby. More and more daddies

mommy info

To cut down on sick days that parents take to care for children, some companies offer discounts on sick-child care at their local children's hospital—or if that's not available in the area, a bonus number of sick days for each employee to cover the necessary time off. For longer illnesses, talk to your human resources manager about the Family Medical Leave Act.

are leaving the rat race to spend time as "house-dads," and they should be applauded for their efforts.

254. Weigh the Benefits of a Home-Based Business

Maybe you've decided that the best option for you is to work your own hours, at your own pace, and still have the luxury of keeping your time with your baby. You want it all, and if you have the right skills, maybe you can have it all. Never has there been a friendlier environment for those who wish to escape the rat race and particularly for those who want to leave the rat race for the things that matter in their lives: their children.

255. Figure Out if It Suits You

Can you work on your own? Have you been self-directed and able to set and accomplish your own goals? Can you perform several tasks at one time? If you can answer yes to any of these questions, you could become an entrepreneur with little or no problem.

If you lack initiative and prefer to have others tell you what to do, you could find yourself in a stress-filled environment within your own walls. Don't take on launching a business if you aren't 100 percent certain you can handle it.

mommy info

Not all companies operate in a discriminatory manner against parents, but you'd be surprised how many still do it subtly. Once employed, it's important to discuss any discrimination concerns with your human resources manager. The Family Medical Leave Act provides some protection for employees with at least one year of eligibility.

256. Make Time for Family

The reality is, both raising a family and developing a business are full-time jobs. So, how can you give 100 percent to each and still maintain your sanity?

First of all, set aside a special time each day or week that is designated as "family time." During this time, don't accept phone calls, don't set appointments, and don't even think about your business. You might not even want to stay near your office. Consider going out to dinner and sharing the three best experiences had by each family member during that week.

257. Stick to Your Commitments

Learn to follow a time-management program. Scheduling your time is the best way to make sure that everything gets done. The rest is just recognizing that it is possible to have two loves: your business and your family.

What should you do in the event that a client or customer wants to meet during one of your special family times? You could rearrange your family time; or, better yet, you could simply say, "I already have a meeting at that time. Is there another time that works for you?" Others will respect your attention to commitments, and you never have to offer any further explanation as to whom you're meeting with.

mommy info

Can you afford to pay self-employment taxes? You will need to do this on a quarterly basis if you choose self-employment. If this is not feasible for you, it may be worth your while to work full- or part-time for someone else and let them worry about the paperwork and taxes.

258. Start Planning Now

Quality day care is in high demand—and some daycare centers even have waiting lists months long. If you wait until after the baby is born, you may have trouble finding a daycare situation you feel totally comfortable with—and waiting too long could mean you'll have to settle for less than your ideal.

Start checking out daycare options as soon as possible—as early as your third month of pregnancy.

259. Find Licensed Centers

Daycare centers are one of the most popular options for working parents. In a center, your child will be cared for in a group setting by adults who are trained in child-rearing and child-development issues. To begin checking into daycare centers, ask your state childcare or child-welfare agency for a list of licensed centers; most states now require commercial childcare providers to be licensed.

260. Check Out the Basics

Call each center on your list for basic info such as fees and availability of space. Ask about the ratio of children to childcare providers. A quality daycare center should care for infants in a separate room, away from toddlers and older children (who can present safety hazards to infants). Infant childcare providers at daycare centers should care for no more than three infants apiece, and two is an even better number.

You should also ask about how many babies are kept in each room. More than six infants in a room, whatever its size, can make for a chaotic setting (and you don't want your baby kept awake constantly from other babies' crying).

261. Pay a Visit

If the center checks out so far, schedule a visit. Here are some things to look for during a visit to a daycare center:

- Do the children at the center seem happy? Do they look reasonably clean?
- Are the rooms bright and airy? Do they have natural light?
- Is there a good selection of toys? Centers should have plenty of age-appropriate, safe toys that encourage creativity and motor development.
- Is the center clean? In particular, check the bathrooms and food preparation areas.
- Is there a safe outdoor play area?
- Is the center thoroughly childproofed? Ask to see fire exits and first aid supplies.

262. Observe the Providers

While you're visiting a daycare center, take the opportunity to watch how the staff interacts with the children and see how they respond to your questions and concerns.

- Do the childcare providers seem attentive to the children's needs?
- How noisy is the center? Happy kids do make noise—but total chaos is a problem.
- Does the staff seem eager to talk with you?
- Are you meeting everyone who works at the facility, from the operator to instructors to cleanup help? You should be able to meet anyone who might possibly come into contact with your baby.

263. Weigh the Negatives

When you are choosing child care for a young infant, you may find daycare centers a bit institutional and potentially over-whelming for your baby. Another negative consideration is the issue of staff turnover. Even good centers can experience a lot of staff turnover, and too many childcare providers in too short a time can interfere with a baby's long-term ability to form last-ing attachments to other people. Finally, any time you take your child outside of your home for care, you are in for a certain amount of inconvenience.

264. Look into Family Day Care

This childcare option is growing in popularity. Unlike a daycare center, a family daycare provider cares for children in her own home. Often, one or more of the children in the group are her own.

Most states have licensing requirements for family day care, but some providers operate illegally, either because they can-not meet the health, safety, or educational requirements of their state licensing agency, or because they do not want to declare their daycare income to the IRS (these will insist that you pay them in cash). If you live in a state that licenses family daycare

mommy info

Being a home-based working parent means you must have a clear sense of priorities. Most likely your family already is a top priority, and work is a close second. However, there will be moments when this order must be reversed. A successful work-at-home parent is able to walk the daily tightrope, achieving this ever-changing balance.

operations, resist the urge to check out that nice, but unlicensed, childcare provider down the street, and only consider licensed childcare providers.

265. Make a List of Family Providers in Your Area

Start your search by obtaining a list of licensed childcare providers in your area from your state childcare or child-welfare agency. Ask friends and neighbors if they know of any good family daycare providers and check to see if those people are on your list. Call those names first and ask if they have room for your child. It can be harder to find family day care for an infant than for a toddler, since childcare providers typically can accept only one or two infants into their group. If a provider is recommended but doesn't have room for your child in the near future, ask her to recommend someone who might.

266. Make an Appointment to Visit

The house where your baby will spend lots of time in the near future should be clean. The kitchen and the bathroom should be sanitary. Also, unless you are standing right next to the diaper pail, you should not detect a strong odor of urine anywhere.

Look carefully at the area in which the children spend most of their time (most likely the living or family room). Is it light and airy? Is the furniture comfortable for small children? Since babies and young children play a lot on the floor, carpeting should be vacuumed frequently, especially if there are pets. The house should also be childproofed, with clearly visible gates on the staircases, latches on kitchen cabinets, and covers on visible electrical outlets.

267. Check References

Check at least three references for a family daycare provider you are considering. If they don't seem enthusiastic about her, keep looking.

In a good family daycare situation, your child will spend her day in a homey atmosphere and will benefit socially by having other children to play with. If you stay with the daycare provider over the long term, your child may come to regard her as a second mom and be treated as part of the family. In many areas of the country, family day care is also relatively inexpensive and a more economical option than are daycare centers. As with a daycare center, though, you sacrifice a certain amount of convenience when you take your children outside your home for child care.

268. Consider In-Home Child Care

When it comes to in-home child care, you have two choices: hire a nanny or an au pair. Each of these offer your child one-on-one attention in your own home and offer the ultimate in convenient child care. Many people think nannies and au pairs are basically the same thing, but there are some important differences.

269. Nannies Generally Have More Experience

A nanny takes care of your child in your home. She may live in your home or live out of it. Many nannies have formal training in child care and child development. Others have no formal training but rely on life experience.

An au pair is typically an eighteen- to twenty-six-year-old foreign student who comes to this country for a year to experience American culture. Au pairs commit to living with a family for a year's time and provide child care and light housework in exchange for room, board, a stipend, and sometimes tuition expenses. Since they are also students, their workload cannot be more than forty-five hours per week.

270. What to Expect from an Agency

There are many agencies that will, for a fee, help you find a nanny. While agencies vary in their screening and training processes, they should, at minimum, do a complete background check of potential candidates (including a police check), provide you with references, and find you at least a couple of candidates to choose from. Fees vary, but in larger cities nanny agencies may charge you fees of $1,000 or more (although if your first choice doesn't work out, the next search may be on the house).

271. Be Prepared to Pay

Nannies are in high demand in most areas and you will need to offer a competitive salary. Live-out nannies working in major metropolitan areas typically earn $14–$20 an hour, depending on their level of experience. For full-time nannies, this can mean a monthly salary of $2,600–$4,000, in addition to medical benefits, paid sick leave, and vacation time, and a variety of other benefits such as health-club membership or travel discounts.

272. If Possible, Opt for a Live-In Nanny

If you're working through a nanny placement service, it's usually the agency that takes care of the nanny's benefits out of the fees you pay them for the nanny's services. You'll pay less if you can find a live-in nanny (you'll need an extra bedroom for this option) who will take part of her compensation as room and board.

273. Be Realistic

Keep your expectations realistic. Outside of hands-on child care, a nanny should be able to prepare your children's meals and perhaps do a little light housework that pertains to their care (like picking up toys or doing your children's laundry). She is not going to clean your house from top to bottom and cook gourmet meals for you while your baby naps.

274. Be Aware of Expectations

If you are considering hiring an au pair, keep in mind that the program was not created to provide child care for Americans. Instead, it was designed to provide a foreign living experience for young people. You should also keep in mind that in other countries, au pairs generally have fewer responsibilities than they are often expected to assume in this country, and they rarely serve as the sole care providers for children while their parents are out of the house.

275. Weight Costs and Benefits

A main attraction of au pairs is cost. If you have an extra bedroom, this is almost always the least expensive childcare option short of relatives. Even when agency fees and an au pair's transportation and tuition are factored in, costs rarely exceed $300 a week, plus room and board, for a maximum of forty-five hours of child care and some light housework. Be aware that while you may end up with a wonderful, nurturing, experienced live-in childcare provider, you may also spend a year trying to train a homesick teenager in the rudiments of baby care. You can always ask for a more experienced au pair prior to making a commitment to the au pair agency.

276. Do Your Own Background Check

If you are not working with a childcare provider network or agency and want to do a background check of local candidates, you can use online services to do so. Start with a search engine such as Google, or visit your local sheriff's website to see their sex offender listing, which (in most cases) can be searched by zip code.

You may also try using some commercial software or web services such as Net Detective, Web Detective, KnowX.com, or LocatePeople.org. To respect privacy laws, it's generally a good idea to get permission in writing from the person you are investigating.

277. The Final Choice Is Yours

With so many childcare choices ahead of you, it's easy to feel overwhelmed. The bottom line is, if you don't feel comfortable—if something about the daycare center or individual childcare provider bothers you, no matter how small or seemingly unimportant—you owe it to yourself to either address the issue or to move on to the next center or person on the list. If you start with a list of most desirable qualities in a childcare provider and rate each one accordingly, a final decision will be much easier to make. The basic things to look for are communication, access, and honesty.

A lot of parents wonder if child-care providers criticize or advise parents on child rearing. The answer is: not unless parents ask for their advice. If asked, they should always offer advice in a noncritical way. Of course, if providers see something that is seriously wrong (i.e., signs of abuse, neglect, or malnutrition), they should discuss the problem with the parents and, if necessary, contact the proper authorities.

278. Set Expectations

Childcare providers should give you frequent and complete updates about your child's progress and problems. If they keep you informed, you can develop ways to deal with problems and build on the activities and accomplishments of the day.

There should always be open access to a home-based or commercial day care. Parents must be welcome to visit at any time, even without calling first. Providers should also allow parents to make a reasonable number of phone calls to check on their child's well-being, especially in the case of minor illness or separation anxiety. You and the provider should work out the best times for these calls and determine in advance how many are reasonable.

If providers feel that they can't abide by certain wishes, they should be candid about their inability to do so. Providers should

mommy info

Always have a backup plan for daycare services! No matter who is supposed to be taking care of your baby—and even if it's you—make sure, if something happens, that you have a backup plan and that that person knows you could call on him/her if you really need it!

159

also abide by parents' wishes on matters such as discipline, TV viewing, food, adult smoking, and toilet training.

279. Request Advance Notice of Changes

Since it is often very difficult to find adequate alternate care, providers should tell parents well in advance if they are going to change their hours or prices—or if they plan to close down or limit the number of children in their care. Parents need at least a month's (or, better yet, six weeks') notice if they need to find a new care provider for their child. A center or family day-care provider should also clarify holiday schedules, so parents know which days are covered and which are not. Not every calendar holiday is a paid holiday for working parents. And except in the case of emergency, parents should be given at least two weeks' notice even if the provider won't be available on a non-holiday day.

280. Stay Connected

Once your baby arrives and you're ready to go back to work, you'll feel a mix of emotions at the prospect of being separated from your child for several hours a day. However, if you've done all of your homework beforehand, you can also feel a strong sense of relief that you've made the best possible choice. Now all you need to do is follow your childcare plan—and find ways to stay connected despite the fact that you are at work.

The best way to remain involved in your child's daycare experience is to stay connected. Set weekly or monthly "in-touch" meetings with your childcare provider to ask questions and discuss your child's progress. Drop in when you can for parties or special events. If getting time away from work is an issue, offer to set up a blog, chat room, or online group where you and your childcare provider can stay in contact throughout the day. Or simply offer to donate snacks, hand sanitizer, or disinfectant for toy cleanup days. With a little effort on your part, you can stay connected to your baby in the most important way of all—ensuring a safe, healthy, and loving "village" of care.

Appendix A

Special Concerns in Pregnancy

The vast majority of American women have an uncomplicated pregnancy. While it's natural to worry about things like miscarriage, preterm birth, and genetic defects, dwelling on every possible thing that could go wrong with your pregnancy can be daunting and self-defeating. This section of *Bottles, Budgets, and Birthplans* is provided as an educational reference. The chances that you will need it are slim, but if you do have problems in pregnancy, staying educated and informed can reduce related stress and help you take the best care of both baby and your body.

Gestational Diabetes

Gestational diabetes mellitus (or diabetes of pregnancy) is caused by a problem processing the glucose (or blood sugar) in your bloodstream. Glucose is important to the body—it provides fuel for cellular growth and metabolism. To be processed effectively, glucose requires a companion hormone known as insulin. Insulin facilitates the transfer of glucose into the cells where it is metabolized (or processed for energy). If there is not enough insulin or if there is insulin that the body isn't using effectively, the result is a backup of glucose into the bloodstream, a situation that is potentially damaging to all of your organ systems and to a developing fetus.

When you develop gestational diabetes, your pancreas is still making plenty of insulin but your body isn't processing it efficiently. The condition, known as insulin resistance, is caused by certain placental hormones that counteract the effect of insulin (for example, estrogen, cortisol, and human placental lactogen, or HPL). In most women, the condition doesn't reach critical levels, and their blood sugar levels stay within normal ranges. In others, excess blood glucose accumulates to potentially dangerous levels and treatment is required.

The Odds

Gestational diabetes mellitus (GDM) occurs in up to 7 percent of all pregnancies in the United States. Factors that may make you more likely to develop GDM include obesity (or high BMI), polyhydramnios (having excess amniotic fluid), a family history of diabetes, a diagnosis of GDM or large birth weight babies in previous pregnancies, and being over age twenty-five.

Diagnosis and Treatment

Diagnosis of GDM is made with the oral glucose tolerance test (OGTT). Because blood sugar levels are influenced by dietary intake, your provider will probably try to treat your GDM with lifestyle and nutritional changes at the onset. A visit with a certified diabetes educator (CDE) and a registered dietitian (RD) can be invaluable in learning more about healthy menu planning, exercise, and the basics of blood sugar control.

You will have to self-test your blood glucose levels on a regular basis with a home meter. The home meter uses a lancet to prick your finger, arm, or another test site for a blood sample. The blood droplet is placed on a test reagent strip that goes into the meter, and the meter provides a blood glucose reading. Testing is generally recommended first thing in the morning (a fasting test) and after meals (postprandial)—usually at one hour and again at two hours after eating. Your doctor may recommend testing at additional times, such as after exercise, if he feels it is warranted. Refer to the table below to see what blood glucose levels the American Diabetes Association recommends for women with gestational diabetes.

Blood Glucose Levels in Women with Gestational Diabetes

Test	Range
Fasting plasma glucose	<105 mg/dl (5.8 mmol/l)
1 hour postprandial plasma glucose	<155 mg/dl (8.6 mmol/l)
2 hour postprandial plasma glucose	<130 mg/dl (7.2 mmol/l)

*Note: mg/dl is the U.S. unit of measure for blood glucose readings, and mmol/l is the international measurement.

If you don't experience significant improvement with dietary changes and your glucose levels still exceed normal ranges, you may have to take insulin injections or medication to keep your blood sugar under control. Injections are typically taken before meals to counteract their impact on glucose levels. Insulin does not cross the placenta and is not harmful to fetal development.

Possible Long-Term Health Effects

Without proper treatment, uncontrolled blood glucose levels can result in fetal death or in a condition known as fetal macrosomia (or a baby that is too large). Blood glucose crosses the placenta in high levels, and the fetus responds by producing more insulin to process the load. The extra glucose is ultimately stored as fat, and the baby potentially grows too large for vaginal birth.

Newborns of GDM moms may also suffer from hypoglycemia at birth (or low blood sugar) as they are suddenly disconnected from the maternal surge of glucose and their high insulin production causes their blood glucose levels to plummet. They may also have an imbalance of blood calcium and blood magnesium levels at birth. Because of these risks, a neonatologist may be on the scene during labor and delivery to treat any potential complications.

Women who develop gestational diabetes have an increased risk of a diagnosis of type 2 diabetes later in life and should receive regular screening for the disease. Their children are also at risk for both type 2 diabetes and obesity. Fortunately, clinical studies have also shown that lifestyle changes involving regular exercise and a healthy diet can be extremely effective in preventing the onset of type 2 diabetes.

Hyperemesis Gravidarum

Hyperemesis gravidarum is excessive nausea and vomiting during pregnancy (that is, morning sickness) that goes beyond the normal gastrointestinal disturbance experienced by many women. Its exact cause is unknown. The condition is diagnosed when nausea and vomiting trigger one or more of the following symptoms:

- Weight loss
- Ketosis/ketonuria
- Dehydration
- Electrolyte imbalance

Other conditions that can cause similar symptoms—including hyperthyroidism, pancreatitis, gall bladder or liver disease, gastritis, appendicitis, and ectopic pregnancy—should be ruled out before diagnosing hyperemesis gravidarum. Treatment typically involves intravenous therapy to rehydrate and encourage weight gain (parenteral nutrition). Hospitalization may be required, and medications may also be prescribed. Infants of mothers who experience this condition are more likely to have lower birth weights and to be small for gestational age.

Fortunately, hyperemesis gravidarum is relatively uncommon, occurring in less than 1 percent of pregnancies.

Incompetent Cervix

An incompetent cervix is a cervix that starts to painlessly open (efface and/or dilate) prematurely. The premature dilatation is not associated with discomfort, contractions, or infection. It may be caused by genetic factors or prior surgeries. If your mother took the drug DES (diethylstilbestrol) when she was pregnant with you, you may also be at risk for an incompetent cervix.

As pregnancy progresses and your unborn child grows and places more pressure on the cervix, without treatment an incompetent cervix may result in miscarriage. Women who have had problems with an incompetent cervix in previous pregnancies are generally offered a prophylactic (or preventative) cerclage in the early second trimester. Cerclage is a minor surgical procedure to suture (stitch) the cervix closed, which may prevent premature cervical opening. There are several different methods of cerclage, including the Shirodkar, the McDonald, and abdominal cerclage. The most common type, the McDonald, is a temporary suture that is removed when labor begins.

A cerclage may also be placed if you have signs of preterm cervical shortening on physical exam or by ultrasound. This is called a *rescue cerclage* and may be less effective than one placed prophylactically. Since it is a controversial topic and a high-risk situation, consultation with a high-risk OB doctor should be made. Women at risk for preterm labor—including those with multiples gestations, those with previous preterm labor, and those with cervical and uterine abnormalities—are generally followed more closely throughout pregnancy.

Women with an incompetent cervix may be regularly monitored using transvaginal ultrasound to detect any cervical changes. Finally, bed rest may be prescribed to keep weight off your uterus, and abstinence from sexual intercourse will probably be recommended.

DES (diethylstilbestrol)

DES daughters, or women who were exposed to the drug DES (diethylstilbestrol) while in their mother's womb, are at risk for an array of health problems. If your mother was treated with DES (which she may be familiar with as synthetic estrogen) between 1940 and 1971, particularly in the first five months of pregnancy, the drug may have affected the development of your reproductive organs. DES daughters are at a higher risk for miscarriage, preterm birth, ectopic pregnancy, and a rare form of cancer called clear cell adenocarcinoma.

Intrauterine Growth Restriction (IUGR)

Intrauterine growth restriction (IUGR) occurs when fetal weight and size gain are estimated to be below the 10th percentile for gestational age. Some IUGR babies may be preterm, but others go to full term. IUGR occurs in up to 10 percent of pregnancies.

Possible causes of IUGR include:

- **Multiples gestations.** IUGR occurs in at least one fetus in up to 20 percent of twins or higher order multiples pregnancies.
- **Infection.** Infectious agents such as toxoplasmosis and cytomegalovirus.
- **Placental problems.** Placenta previa, accreta, or abruption, along with other placental abnormalities.
- **Maternal hypertension.** High blood pressure in pregnancy, including preeclampsia.
- **Maternal tobacco, alcohol, and drug use.** Smoking moms-to-be are almost twice as likely as nonsmokers to have a low birth weight baby.
- **Poor maternal nutrition.** Malnutrition and inadequate protein intake can restrict fetal growth and may lead to adult health problems such as hypertension and insulin resistance later in life.
- **Genetic anomalies.** Arrested physical and mental growth is one of the features of many chromosomal disorders, including Down Syndrome and Edwards Syndrome (Trisomy 21 and Trisomy 18).
- **Birth defects.** Birth defects such as a congenital heart or kidney malformation may restrict blood flow and affect fetal growth.

- **Altitude.** The reduced oxygen supply at high elevations decreases blood flow to the uterus and placenta and is thought to be a factor in IUGR and low birth weight.
- **Certain chronic illnesses.** Maternal heart disease, sickle cell disease, diabetes, and systemic lupus erythematosis (SLE, or lupus), among others.

A fundal height (uterus height) that is measuring too small for the due date is the first tipoff to IUGR. An ultrasound can give your provider an idea of actual fetal size, and if IUGR is diagnosed you will probably be undergoing regular ultrasounds, nonstress tests, and biophysical profiles through the remainder of pregnancy to follow your baby's progress. IUGR pregnancies are at risk for intrapartum asphyxia (blocked oxygen flow to fetus), oligohydramnios (low amniotic fluid volume), and possible preterm birth and its related complications. At birth IUGR babies are at risk for a number of medical problems, including high blood pressure, hypoglycemia (low blood sugar), anemia, polycythemia (an excess of red blood cells), neurological problems, and jaundice. Later in life they may experience some developmental problems. Low birth weight (LBW), including both IUGR and preterm LBW, is the leading cause of infant mortality in the United States.

IUGR that begins early in pregnancy and affects the fetal body uniformly is said to be symmetric. Symmetric IUGR may be caused by genetic abnormality, fetal infection, or exposure to teratogen. Growth restriction that occurs later in pregnancy and is thought to be caused by insufficient fetal nutrition is termed *asymmetric IUGR*. It is also called *head sparing IUGR* because the fetus has focused its limited resources on vital brain development, making the head in these babies much larger than the body. Asymmetric IUGR infants typically have a better prognosis or long-term outlook.

Placenta Problems

The placenta provides nourishment, blood, and oxygen to your baby and is literally what connects the two of you. Problems can occur with either the structure or the placement of the placenta, which may pose a risk to you and to your unborn child.

Uteroplacental Insufficiency (UPI)

Uteroplacental insufficiency occurs when the blood flow and consequently oxygen supply from mother to fetus is impaired or inadequate in some way. This is usually the result of an acute or chronic maternal illness (for example, hypertension, diabetes, preeclampsia, kidney disease), although it can arise from chromosomal abnormalities in the fetus. It may also occur in cases of multiples gestation (that is, twins, triplets, or more).

Clinical signs that UPI may be present include:

- Oligohydramnios. Low levels of amniotic fluid, apparent on ultrasound.
- A nonreactive nonstress test (NST). If the fetus is hypoxic (getting insufficient oxygen), its heart rate will not accelerate with (or react to) fetal movement.
- Late decelerations in a stress test (or contraction stress test). A slowdown in fetal heart rate that peaks toward the end of a contraction also indicates hypoxia.
- Intrauterine growth restriction (IUGR; see above). A fetus that is small for gestational age on ultrasound.

If you are diagnosed with UPI, steps will be taken to correct or treat the underlying cause, if possible. Fetal distress may be cause for immediate cesarean delivery.

Placenta Previa

A placenta that implants and grows near or covering the cervical opening (or os) occurs in an estimated one of every 200 pregnancies in the second trimester. This condition, called *placenta previa,* often resolves itself as the uterus enlarges about 90 percent of the time. However, if placenta previa persists late in pregnancy, a potentially life-threatening hemorrhage can occur when the cervix starts to efface (thin) and dilate (open).

Placenta previa may be total (that is, completely covering the os), partial (that is, partially covering the os), or marginal (that is, on the margin, or edge, of the os). The condition is diagnosed by ultrasound. Vaginal bleeding is a possible symptom, but some women have no symptoms whatsoever.

If bleeding does occur, bed rest may be prescribed. Blood transfusion may also be necessary. Women who have placenta previa will usually require a cesarean delivery.

Low-Lying Placenta

A low-lying placenta is a placenta that is near the os but not close enough to be considered marginal. Like placenta previa, this type of placental implantation has a higher risk of bleeding during late pregnancy.

If you are diagnosed with a low-lying placenta in the first or second trimester, there's a good chance that the placenta will reposition itself as the uterus expands. Because the cervix begins to thin (or efface) during the third trimester, if the placenta remains low in the uterus, hemorrhage becomes a risk.

Women who still have a low-lying placenta in the third trimester are usually prescribed bed rest, and a cesarean section may be recommended.

Placental Abruption

Vaginal bleeding, abdominal cramping, and symptoms of shock (that is, irregular heartbeat, low blood pressure, pale complexion) in the second and third trimesters may indicate that the placenta has begun to prematurely separate from the wall of the uterus, a condition called *placental abruption* (or *abruptio placenta*). Risk factors for placental abruption include maternal high blood pressure, cocaine use, or physical trauma to the abdomen.

Abruption may occur anytime after week 20, and if you have had a previous occurrence in an earlier pregnancy, your risk of experiencing it again is increased. Placental abruption may cause major life-threatening hemorrhage, fetal distress or possibly death, and preterm labor. However, a swift diagnosis and initiation of treatment, including blood transfusion, IV fluids, and oxygen, can do much to improve outcomes. Immediate delivery, possibly by C-section, is indicated in the majority of cases but depends on the stability of both mother and fetus and the length of gestation. In some cases in which only a small segment of the placenta prematurely separates from the uterine wall, careful maternal and fetal monitoring and bed rest may carry a pregnancy safely to term.

Placenta Accreta

Placenta accreta occurs when the placenta implants or attaches to the myometrium (or uterine muscle) instead of to the endometrium. Placenta accreta can be further categorized into two subtypes based on the extent of myometrium invasion—placenta increta and placenta percreta.

In pregnancy complicated by placenta accreta, the placenta does not easily separate from the uterine wall during the third stage of delivery, and postpartum hemorrhage (PPH) occurs. A postpartum blood transfusion, arterial embolization, or an emergency hysterectomy (surgical removal of the uterus) may be required to stop the bleeding and stabilize the patient. If you are diagnosed with this condition prior to delivery, it's important to discuss the possibility of a hysterectomy. In many clinical situations, a hysterectomy may be unavoidable, but if an option is available, your doctor needs to know of any desire for more children so she can preserve your fertility if at all possible.

According to the ACOG, the incidence of placenta accreta has risen dramatically in the past fifty years and currently happens at a rate of one in every 2,500 deliveries. This increase can probably be traced to the climb in cesarean section rates; placenta accreta is more likely to occur in women with a history of cesarean delivery (and climbs with each subsequent C-section). In addition, women who are diagnosed with placenta previa have a substantially increased risk of placenta accreta.

If you are considered at risk for the condition, magnetic resonance imaging (MRI) and ultrasound may be used to confirm a diagnosis. A high alpha-fetoprotein (AFP) level may also be a sign of placenta accreta.

Preeclampsia/Eclampsia

Gestational hypertension, or otherwise uncomplicated high blood pressure of pregnancy occurring after 20 weeks of gestation, appears in up to 10 percent of pregnancies. When high blood pressure in pregnancy is accompanied by proteinuria (protein in the urine) and edema (swelling), it is known as pre-eclampsia. Symptoms of preeclampsia include:

- High blood pressure (140/90 or higher)
- Excessive swelling of hands and/or feet
- Sudden weight gain
- Protein in the urine
- Blurry vision
- Abdominal pain (usually on the upper right side)
- Headache

Preeclampsia typically happens in the third trimester. If characterized as mild, it may be controlled by bed rest, medication, and careful monitoring of the fetus. Hospitalization may be required. If the pregnancy has reached week 37, delivery may be induced or performed via C-section to avoid further risk.

If the preeclampsia worsens or is severe, delivery may be required earlier than week 37. In some cases seizures may develop, which indicates that preeclampsia has progressed to eclampsia. Eclampsia is rare but potentially life-threatening, and your physician will weigh the risks and benefits to you and your baby when deciding when delivery is right in preterm pregnancies.

Premature Labor

Delivery of your baby after week 20 and before week 37 of pregnancy is considered preterm or premature. In cases of very early preterm labor where fetal lung maturity hasn't been established, your provider will probably try to delay the delivery for as long as possible. Preemies can suffer from a wide range of physical, neurological, and developmental difficulties, so any extra time spent in the womb is beneficial.

Are You at Risk?

A number of environmental and physical factors have been associated with an increased chance of preterm delivery. These include but are not limited to:

- Previous premature labor
- Pregnant with multiples (twins or more)
- Brief period of time between pregnancies
- Previous uterine surgery
- Hypertension (high blood pressure)
- Cigarette smoking
- Diagnosed incompetent cervix
- Drug or alcohol abuse
- Vaginal or systemic infection
- Obesity
- Being underweight prepregnancy
- Blood clotting disorders
- Exposure to drug DES
- Domestic violence
- Lack of appropriate prenatal care
- Working more than forty hours a week and/or standing more than six hours per day

Women at high risk for preterm birth (for example, those who have had a previous spontaneous preterm birth) may be given regular injections of the hormone progesterone administered in the second and third trimesters to cut the risk of preterm labor.

Warning Signs

If you experience any of the following warning signs of pre-term labor, call your healthcare provider immediately. If you are out of town or unable to get in touch with her for any reason, go directly to the nearest hospital emergency room. With prompt action, it may be possible to delay your labor until your unborn child has adequate time to develop.

Symptoms include:

- Painful contractions at regular intervals
- Abdominal cramps
- Lower backache
- Bloody vaginal discharge
- Stomach pain
- Any type of fluid leak from the vagina, large or small

Treatment

Preterm labor may be halted by bed rest, tocolytic medications (drugs that stop contractions), and intravenous hydration. Depending on your medical history and how far along your pregnancy is, you may be hospitalized. Home bed rest may also be prescribed, and you might be required to hook up to a fetal monitor on a regular basis. If preterm labor occurs between 24 and 34 weeks, corticosteroids may be administered to hasten fetal lung surfactant development as well.

If your cervix dilates to 4 or 5 centimeters or if your fetus is showing signs of distress, preterm delivery may be unavoidable.

A level-three neonatal intensive care unit (NICU) is the best place for your newborn to receive treatment if he is delivered preterm. These units are highly experienced in the care of high-risk newborns and preemies and have state-of-the-art technology and training. The American Academy of Pediatrics and the American College of Obstetricians and Gynecologists recommend that all deliveries that occur earlier than week 32 take place at these facilities.

Preterm Premature Rupture of Membranes (PPROM)

Premature rupture of the amniotic membrane is not necessarily a problem if it occurs late in pregnancy. However, when it happens before week 37 of gestation, certain steps should be taken to ensure that your fetus has enough time for development in the womb.

PPROM may occur in women at risk for preterm labor. Other possible causes of PPROM include cervical incompetence and vaginal infection. If PPROM occurs prior to week 32, bed rest and frequent fetal heart monitoring may be recommended in an effort to prolong pregnancy until the fetal lungs mature. Antibiotics are administered to ward off infection in both fetus and mother, and steroids may be prescribed to speed lung surfactant production in the fetus. If PPROM occurs after weeks 34 to 35, your physician will probably recommend inducing your labor since the risks of infection are usually higher than the risks of a premature delivery.

Choroid Plexus Cysts

Ultrasound technology has become so advanced in recent years that it is able to pick up more anomalies earlier and earlier, anomalies that statistically tend to mean nothing in most low-risk pregnancies. One of these anomalies may be choroid plexus cysts—small cysts appearing on the choroid of the fetal brain.

If no other abnormalities are seen on the scan, choroid plexus cysts have an excellent chance of resolving themselves by around week 24 with no ill effects to your child. The cysts are of note because in a small number of cases they have been associated with the serious chromosomal abnormality trisomy 18 (Edward's syndrome). A meeting with a genetic counselor will help you weigh the risks and benefits of further testing in your particular situation.

Ectopic Pregnancy

Ectopic pregnancy occurs when implantation takes place outside of the endometrial lining. In the majority of cases, it occurs in the fallopian tube, which is why it is often referred to as a tubal pregnancy. However, an ectopic pregnancy may also implant in the ovary, cervix, abdominal cavity, or cornual portion of the uterus (close to the fallopian tubes).

Unfortunately, pregnancy implantation must occur in the endometrium of the uterus for a pregnancy to safely continue. Allowing a pregnancy to progress in the fallopian tube or other ectopic site will result in tubal or other rupture in the first trimester, unavoidable fetal death, and potential maternal death. If you are diagnosed with an ectopic pregnancy, it will need to be surgically removed or treated with the drug methotrexate. Early treatment can preserve your fertility for subsequent pregnancies.

Women who have had previous ectopic pregnancies, who become pregnant with an IUD contraceptive device in place, who have a history of endometriosis and/or pelvic inflammatory disease (PID), and who have had a tubal ligation procedure are at a higher risk for ectopic pregnancy. The March of Dimes estimates that one in fifty pregnancies are ectopic.

Early signs of ectopic pregnancy include low hCG levels or abnormally rising hCG levels (hCG should approximately double every two days in a normal pregnancy), abdominal pain, and irregular bleeding. An abdominal or transvaginal ultrasound can usually confirm the diagnosis. If it remains undiagnosed, ectopic pregnancy is potentially life-threatening and can endanger future fertility. Warning signs that an undetected ectopic pregnancy may have ruptured include:

- Severe abdominal and/or pelvic pain
- Vaginal bleeding
- Dizziness
- Shoulder pain
- Nausea and vomiting

If you experience any of these symptoms, seek medical care immediately.

Molar Pregnancy

Like an ectopic pregnancy, a molar pregnancy is also not viable. However, in a molar pregnancy, the implantation site is normal but the embryo is not. Called a hydatidiform mole, this placental tissue develops into a mass of cysts that are often described as resembling a cluster of grapes. There are two types of molar pregnancy, complete and incomplete (or partial).

A complete molar pregnancy occurs when an egg with no genetic material inside is fertilized by one or two sperm. Most have forty-six chromosomes, all from the father (paternal). The pregnancy itself contains placental mass only and no embryonic tissue.

A partial molar pregnancy will usually contain some embryonic or fetal tissue. The majority of partial molar cases have two sets of paternal chromosomes and a single set of maternal chromosomes (sixty-nine in total).

Symptoms of molar pregnancy include:

- Too small or too large uterus for date
- Enlarged ovaries
- Possible high hCG levels
- Dark brown bleeding in the first trimester
- Preeclampsia and toxemia

Ultrasound can make a diagnosis of molar pregnancy, which is estimated to occur in approximately one in 1,500 pregnancies in the United States. Older women have a higher risk for the condition, and the risk of subsequent molar pregnancy increases with each occurrence.

Risk of molar pregnancy is also influenced by geography. Although the incidence of the condition in the United States is relatively low, about one in 120 pregnancies in Southeastern Asia is molar. Several studies have also shown a higher incidence of molar pregnancy among women in the Philippines and Mexico. The exact reasons behind this phenomenon aren't completely understood, although genetic factors, diet, and environment have all been proposed as possible influences.

Removal by dilation and curettage (D & C) is the typical treatment for molar pregnancy. D & C is a surgical procedure involving dilating the cervix and suctioning the contents of the uterus. Synthetic hormones (oxytocin) may also be administered during the procedure to induce uterine contractions.

A molar pregnancy has the potential to develop into a rare type of cancer known as choriocarcinoma. A chest X-ray, blood-work, and other radiological exams are done prior to D&C to determine if a molar pregnancy has metastasized (spread to other parts of the body).

Followup blood tests may be required for six months to a year afterwards to ensure that hCG levels have returned to normal. Levels that fail to return to normal or start to rise are an indication that persistent gestational trophoblastic disease (GTD) is present and further treatment is necessary. Rarely GTD may develop into choriocarcinoma. To accurately screen for these possibilities and ensure an early diagnosis, subsequent pregnancy should be avoided until the followup period is complete. Survival and remission rates are good if GTD is caught early and treated appropriately.

Miscarriage

Up to 20 percent of all detected pregnancies miscarry before week 20 of gestation. A miscarriage may also be referred to as a spontaneous abortion or a missed abortion. Approximately half of all miscarriages are caused by chromosomal or genetic abnormalities, while in the other half the cause remains unclear.

Other factors to be considered in a miscarriage are:

- Hormonal deficiencies
- Abnormalities of the cervix or uterus
- Incompatible blood types or the Rh factor
- Viruses and infections
- Immune disorders

Warning Signs

Some of the warning signs of miscarriage can also happen in perfectly normal and healthy pregnancies. Light blood spotting, for example, is a common occurrence in pregnancy when implantation takes place. Do take any symptoms seriously and contact your provider as soon as they occur, but keep in mind that the appearance of blood spots or minor cramping doesn't guarantee miscarriage.

Signs and symptoms of miscarriage may include:

- Bright red vaginal bleeding
- Abdominal cramping
- Low back pain
- High fever
- Extreme nausea and vomiting that's sudden and unusual
- Amniotic fluid leakage
- Severe headache

Some women panic when they experience a sudden improvement in previously troublesome pregnancy symptoms. Remember that this is a common phenomenon toward the end of the first trimester as hormone levels start to balance out. If you're still concerned or something just doesn't feel quite right, call your provider to schedule a quick appointment for a listen to the fetal heartbeat. Most will be happy to comply to ease your mind.

Coping with Loss

It doesn't take long to fall hopelessly in love with your unborn child, to dream about your future together, and to start making a special place within your family for him or her. "Love at first thought" is perhaps the most accurate way to describe how many moms and dads feel about it.

That is what makes pregnancy loss so difficult at any point in the process. You may hear insensitive comments like, "Well, at least you were only a few weeks along" that are meant to be sympathetic but only serve to minimize the very real grief you are experiencing. Give yourself adequate time to mourn and to deal with the feelings of anger, guilt, frustration, and depression. Talk to your doctor about a referral to a pregnancy loss support group or to a one-on-one counselor or therapist. You may also want to visit the Hygeia Foundation for Perinatal Loss, Inc. for online support and information at *www.hygeia.org*.

It's extremely important to take care of yourself during this difficult time. If you hadn't yet told anyone about the pregnancy at the point miscarriage occurred, it may be tougher to find enough time to reflect and grieve. Allow yourself to take a few sick or personal days off of work to spend healing time with your significant other and family. Don't rush things.

Trying Again

When to try again is a delicate issue. You need to be ready both emotionally and physically. Make sure you have had time to grieve your loss, and consult with your provider about the causes behind your first miscarriage. Your provider might recommend that you wait for a period to allow your body time to recover. If you do want to try again immediately, make sure you express your wishes so you both can prepare properly for the next time around.

Most miscarriages occur due to factors completely beyond anyone's control—a defective egg or sperm, implantation outside the endometrium. Other triggers, such as teratogen exposure, may be avoided with special precautions in pregnancy. Definitely speak with your healthcare provider about your concerns and any special instructions given your medical history (for example, activity restrictions).

If you've experienced repeated miscarriage, considered clinically to be three consecutive pregnancy losses before week 20, further investigation is in order before attempting another pregnancy. The cause can sometimes be determined by a pathological examination of the miscarried fetus or embryo. A meeting with a genetic counselor, and a full preconception diagnostic workup to examine your fallopian tubes, uterus, and other possible sites of a problem may also be recommended.

Worksheets and Checklists

On the following pages, you will find some worksheets and checklists. Fill these out before you go to the doctor—this way you won't forget to mention anything about your health history.

personal medical history worksheet

Fill out your personal medical history here so you can easily answer the questions your doctor asks you at your first visit.

Chronic illnesses

_____

_____

_____

_____

Current medications

_____

_____

_____

_____

Current vitamins, dietary supplements, and herbal supplements

_____

_____

_____

_____

_____

_____

Allergies to medications

_____

_____

_____

_____

Past surgeries

_____

_____

_____

_____

Tobacco use (include frequency of use)

_____

Average number of alcoholic beverages consumed per week

_____

Current level of physical activity

_____

_____

_____

Have you had:	Yes	No
Seizure disorder	O	O
Epilepsy	O	O
Insomnia	O	O
Frequent anxiety	O	O
Frequent depression	O	O
Recurrent headache	O	O
Asthma	O	O
Pain/pressure in chest	O	O
Chronic cough	O	O
Palpitations (heart)	O	O
Valvular, congenital, or other heart disease	O	O
High or low blood pressure	O	O
Rheumatic fever or heart murmur	O	O
Back problems	O	O
Tumor, cancer, cyst	O	O
Jaundice (liver disease)	O	O
Stomach or intestinal trouble	O	O
Mononucleosis	O	O
Gallbladder trouble or gallstones	O	O
Recurrent diarrhea	O	O
Hernia	O	O
Recent weight gain/loss	O	O
Dizziness, fainting	O	O
Weakness, paralysis	O	O
Blood clots	O	O
Thyroid disorders	O	O

Have you had:	Yes	No
Urinary tract infections or kidney disease	O	O
Bowel disease	O	O
Significant hemorrhoids	O	O
Blood transfusion	O	O
Albumin-sugar in urine	O	O
Blood in urine	O	O
Diabetes	O	O
Peptic ulcer	O	O
Collagen disease	O	O
Pneumonia	O	O
Irregular periods	O	O
Severe cramps	O	O
Excessive menstrual flow	O	O

Sexually Transmitted Diseases   Treatment
(past and present, if any)

_____

_____

_____

_____

Fertility issues (if any)   Treatment

_____

_____

_____

_____

Number of previous pregnancies

_____

In previous pregnancy, have you experienced:	Yes	No
Birth weights less than 2,500 grams	○	○
Birth weights greater than 4,000 grams	○	○
Preterm labor	○	○
Preterm rupture of membranes before onset of labor	○	○
Complications with labor or delivery	○	○
Pregnancy-induced hypertension	○	○
Preeclampsia	○	○
Postpartum hemorrhage	○	○
Third-trimester bleeding	○	○
Anemia	○	○
Miscarriage	○	○
Stillbirth	○	○
Abortion	○	○
Neonatal death	○	○

Previous miscarriage or abortion   Date of miscarriage or abortion

_____

_____

_____

Other complications during previous pregnancies   Treatments

_____

_____

_____

family medical history worksheet

Medical Condition	No	Yes	Do Not Know	Relationship
Diabetes	○	○	○	_____
Hypertension	○	○	○	_____
Psychiatric disorders	○	○	○	_____
Alcoholism	○	○	○	_____
Neural tube defects	○	○	○	_____
Multiple births	○	○	○	_____
Macrosomia	○	○	○	_____
Congenital defects	○	○	○	_____
Hearing problems	○	○	○	_____
Cleft palate or lip	○	○	○	_____
Sickle cell anemia	○	○	○	_____
Hemophilia	○	○	○	_____
Downs Syndrome	○	○	○	_____
Cystic Fibrosis	○	○	○	_____
Huntington's Chorea	○	○	○	_____
Cerebral palsy	○	○	○	_____
Muscular dystrophy	○	○	○	_____
Nerve-muscle disorder	○	○	○	_____
Thyroid disorder	○	○	○	_____
Other hormonal disorder	○	○	○	_____
Dwarfism	○	○	○	_____
Hepatitis B, C, or carrier	○	○	○	_____
Blindness, visual problems	○	○	○	_____
Hand or feet abnormalities	○	○	○	_____
Autism	○	○	○	_____
Miscarriage	○	○	○	_____
Lou Gehrig's Disease	○	○	○	_____

Medical Condition	No	Yes	Do Not Know	Relationship
Cancer	○	○	○	_____
Endometriosis	○	○	○	_____
Sudden Infant Death Syndrome	○	○	○	_____

Other

_____

_____

_____

_____

_____

_____

_____

_____

_____

_____

_____

_____

_____

_____

_____

prenatal visit notes

Stats

Weight _____

Week of Pregnancy _____

Fundal height _____

Blood pressure _____

Baby's heart rate _____

Tests

Test   *Result*

_____   _____

_____   _____

_____   _____

_____   _____

_____   _____

Additional Notes

_____

_____

_____

_____

_____

Common Tests

Over the course of your pregnancy, you'll be visiting your healthcare provider quite a bit. Your provider will administer a number of tests to make sure that you and your baby remain healthy throughout your pregnancy, and that neither you or your baby are at risk for complications.

Following are the most common tests you will undergo and what they test for.

Urine culture
Tests for presence of ketones and levels of protein, bacteria and glucose

Rh factor *(Rh positive or negative)*
If you are Rh negative, you are at risk for Rh incompatibility with the blood type of your baby

Hemoglobin/hematocrit
Tests for anemia

Glucose challenge test
Tests for gestational diabetes mellitus *(GDM)*

Oral Glucose Tolerance Test *(GTT)*
Provides definitive diagnosis of GDM

Hepatitis B
Tests for the presence of Hepatitis B in the blood

Pap smear
Detects cervical cancer, precancerous cells, vaginal infections, or inflammation of the cervix

Chorionic villus sampling *(CVS)*
Tests for Down syndrome and more than 200 other disorders

Alpha-fetoprotein *(AFP)* blood tests *(or variations called the triple or quad AFP screens)*
Screens for chromosomal irregularities like trisomy 18 and Down syndrome, and for neural tube defects

Cystic Fibrosis screening
Screens to see if you are a carrier

Amniocentesis
Diagnoses chromosomal abnormalities, genetic disorders, and birth defects

Ultrasounds
May be used to diagnose placental abnormalities, an ectopic pregnancy, or certain birth defects

labor and delivery

Time of first contraction: _____

Where you were when labor began: _____

Date admitted: _____

Time admitted: _____

Delivery date: _____

Delivery time: _____

Baby's length: _____

Baby's weight: _____

Any complications during labor and delivery: _____

_____

_____

_____

Additional information about delivery: _____

_____

_____

_____

_____

_____

_____

_____

items for leaving the house

Once you and your baby are home from the hospital, you'll need a few items so that you can pay visits to friends and family (and be out and about) with everything you'll need to keep you and your baby comfortable. Some items you might consider purchasing are:

- Stroller
- Jogging stroller
- Diaper bag
- Backpack or convertible backpack/frontpack
- Car seat
- Toy for car seat
- Sling
- Sunshade

Additional Items to Buy

_____

_____

_____

_____

_____

_____

_____

_____

_____

_____

_____

Appendix B

A Nine-Month Checklist

Here's a checklist of things to do during your pregnancy. Have fun while preparing for your little one!

month one checklist

○ Evaluate your doctor, midwife, or group practice and decide if it's right for you and your pregnancy.

○ Discuss any possible on-the-job hazards with your doctor or midwife.

○ Evaluate your diet and begin taking prenatal vitamins if recommended by your doctor or midwife.

○ Get up to speed on your health insurance coverage for prenatal visits, delivery, and the care of your child.

○ If you smoke or drink, quit now.

month two checklist

○ Start developing a maternity wardrobe.

○ Make room for your baby.

○ Make sleep a priority; set a new early bedtime and stick to it.

month three checklist

○ Prepare a budget to save for when your baby arrives.

○ Inform your employer.

○ Get details on your maternity benefits.

○ Look into a prenatal exercise class.

○ Decide where the baby's room or space will be.

○ Share the good news with your other kids.

month four checklist

○ Treat yourself to a special day out.

○ Begin keeping a food log.

○ If you don't have one, shop for a crib that meets current safety standards.

○ Create a prenatal exercise routine.

○ Find out how and when to add your new baby to your insurance coverage.

○ Do some basic babyproofing.

month five checklist

○ Plan a special night out with your partner.

○ Choose a method of childbirth instruction.

○ Tour childbirth centers.

○ Create a baby-safe car environment.

○ Ensure that your vehicle is child-seat friendly.

○ Purchase a rear-facing infant seat for your child.

○ Try your hand at properly installing it in your vehicle.

○ Explore childcare options for your new baby.

month six checklist

○ Take a day off and pamper yourself.

○ Start putting together your birth plan.

○ Think about whom you want in the delivery room.

○ Begin listing baby names.

○ Discuss your maternity leave plans with your employer.

month seven checklist

○ Make a date with yourself to relax, read, or just catch up on sleep.

○ Interview pediatricians.

○ Sign up for childbirth classes.

○ Sign your child up for sibling classes.

○ Contemplate the breast-versus-bottle decision.

○ Set up an appointment to discuss your birth plan with your provider.

○ Arrange for care for your other children during your hospital stay.

month eight checklist

○ Take five and de-stress; it's good for you and baby.

○ Lay out your baby's essentials.

○ Compare and decide on cloth versus disposable diapers.

○ Discuss circumcision with your pediatrician and your partner.

○ Start wrapping up projects at work.

○ Finalize your childcare plans for after maternity leave.

○ Preregister at your hospital or birthing center.

month nine checklist

○ Make sure that your other children's teachers and care providers are aware of your impending hospital stay.

○ Pack your bag and compile a call list for your partner.

○ Line up postpartum assistance.

○ Stock up the freezer with heat-and-eat meals or recruit postpartum kitchen help.

○ Make a plan and a backup plan for getting to the hospital.

○ Put your feet up, relax, and take a deep breath. The rest is up to your baby!

Appendix C

Additional Resources

Websites for Expectant and New Parents

The following sites were created especially with pregnant couples and new parents in mind.

About—Pregnancy & Childbirth

http://pregnancy.about.com

This highly informative site includes information on everything from conception to postpartum issues. Other very cool features include an ultrasound gallery and a week-by-week pregnancy calendar to guide you through each phase of your pregnancy.

Baby Bag Online

www.babybag.com

A plethora of pregnancy, childbirth, and parenting tips—plus recipes, product and book reviews, and message boards created for specific subgroups. There's also an online store.

BabyCenter

www.babycenter.com

This site features lots of great articles on a variety of topics for expectant and new parents. Check out the due date calculator, as well as the pregnancy calendar designed for tracking your baby's growth throughout and beyond your pregnancy—week by precious week.

Pampers.com

www.pampers.com

Expert information, product features, and lots of great tips for new parents.

Parenting

The following sites contain broad, general parenting tips and advice—mostly from other parents, though some carry articles written by experts.

About—Parenting & Family

www.about.com/parenting

Everything you want to know about parenting, family life, baby products, fatherhood, special needs, and stay-at-home parenting—plus the latest information on product recalls.

iVillage Parenting

http://parenting.ivillage.com

Full of great parenting tips from experts as well as other parents, this popular site includes an online community for more interactivity with others who've been there and lived to tell.

KidSource OnLine

www.kidsource.com

Lots of information for parents of children from newbies to school-aged. Find what you're looking for by choosing sections of specific interest and then perusing the many articles contained in each section.

Parenthood.com

www.parenthood.com

Subscribe to this free e-newsletter and you'll have instant access to hundreds of articles written by experts. You can add your own comments, or simply read others' comments in the reader's forum. If you want, you can also participate in surveys or in live chats.

Urbanbaby.com

www.urbanbaby.com

Comprehensive resource guides and interactive communities in seven major metropolitan areas, including Austin, Boston, Chicago, Los Angeles, New York, San Francisco, and Seattle. Sign up for the Urban Baby Daily to receive regular tips, new product information, and more.

Zero to Three

www.zerotothree.com

This site offers both professional and parents' sections, and provides insights into child development. If you're wondering whether your baby's on track, this will be a valuable resource for you.

Parent's Resource Center

The National Parenting Center

www.tnpc.com

Get age-specific advice from the experts, who focus on distinct stages of child development.

Sesame Street Parents

www.ctw.org/parents

Produced by the Children's Television Workshop (the same great folks who bring you TV's *Sesame Street*), this informative site offers content on everything from health and safety tips to education and community. One added bonus is an activities area featuring fun and educational things to do together.

Parent News

www.parent.net

Here you'll find lots of articles, tips, and news-related content on a wide variety of issues and topics of importance to you as a new (or even experienced) parent.

Especially for Moms

Working Mother

www.workingmother.com

If you work outside of your home, this site offers lots of great content for you. You'll appreciate advice on career strategies and finding balance, as well as the links to other resources.

Moms on the Move

www.momsonthemove.com

An uplifting site for moms who seek reassurance that their lives are larger than their families. Visit this site to read inspiring stories of other moms who have somehow managed to have it all.

Especially for Dads

National Fatherhood Initiative

www.fatherhood.org

This established group for fathers offers dads terrific support through events, programs, online resources, and a national educational campaign. But you can also find great tools for rating companies and local programs for "dad-friendliness."

Fathers.com

www.fathers.com

This site was created by the National Center for Fathering, and is a fantastic resource for dads who want to be very involved in their kids' lives. Check out all of the tips and training-related content.

Health Care

Mayo Clinic

www.mayoclinic.com

The world-renowned Mayo Clinic is your expert source for health information on everything from pregnancy to child and family health. Go to the "Healthy Living Center" for informative articles on several topics.

KidsHealth.org

www.kidshealth.org/index.html

Sponsored by the Nemours Foundation, this site offers a section for parents as well as kids and includes a search engine to make finding your topic that much easier.

Healthfinder

www.healthfinder.gov

Free health information from the U.S. government is at your fingertips through this consumer-oriented gateway site. Quickly and easily find links to the latest health news, events, and press releases, as well as online journals. You can also locate toll-free numbers and self-help and support group information here.

WomensHealth.gov

www.4women.gov/pregnancy

Here, you'll find Getting Ready for Baby fact sheets and links to other free, informative government resources.

Appendix D

Baby Names

Baby Names Throughout the Ages

top ten names of the 1880s

Boys	Girls
1. John	1. Mary
2. William	2. Anna
3. Charles	3. Elizabeth
4. George	4. Margaret
5. James	5. Minnie
6. Joseph	6. Emma
7. Frank	7. Martha
8. Henry	8. Alice
9. Thomas	9. Marie
10. Harry	10. Annie, Sarah (tie)

top ten names of the 1890s

Boys	Girls
1. John	1. Mary
2. William	2. Anna
3. James	3. Elizabeth
4. George	4. Emma
5. Charles	5. Margaret
6. Joseph	6. Rose
7. Frank	7. Ethel
8. Harry	8. Florence
9. Henry	9. Ida
10. Edward	10. Bertha, Helen (tie)

top ten names of the 1900s

Boys	Girls
1. John	1. Mary
2. William	2. Helen
3. James	3. Margaret
4. George	4. Anna
5. Joseph	5. Ruth
6. Charles	6. Elizabeth
7. Robert	7. Dorothy
8. Frank	8. Marie
9. Edward	9. Mildred
10. Henry	10. Alice

top ten names of the 1910s

Boys	Girls
1. John	1. Mary
2. William	2. Helen
3. James	3. Dorothy
4. Robert	4. Margaret
5. Joseph	5. Ruth
6. George	6. Mildred
7. Charles	7. Anna
8. Edward	8. Elizabeth
9. Frank	9. Frances
10. Thomas	10. Virginia

top ten names of the 1920s

Boys	Girls
1. Robert	1. Mary
2. John	2. Dorothy
3. James	3. Helen
4. William	4. Betty
5. Charles	5. Margaret
6. George	6. Ruth
7. Joseph	7. Virginia
8. Richard	8. Doris
9. Edward	9. Mildred
10. Donald	10. Elizabeth

top ten names of the 1930s

Boys	Girls
1. Robert	1. Mary
2. James	2. Betty
3. John	3. Barbara
4. William	4. Shirley
5. Richard	5. Patricia
6. Charles	6. Dorothy
7. Donald	7. Joan
8. George	8. Margaret
9. Thomas	9. Nancy
10. Joseph	10. Helen

top ten names of the 1940s

Boys	Girls
1. James	1. Mary
2. Robert	2. Linda
3. John	3. Barbara
4. William	4. Patricia
5. Richard	5. Carol
6. David	6. Sandra
7. Charles	7. Nancy
8. Thomas	8. Judith
9. Michael	9. Sharon
10. Ronald	10. Susan

top ten names of the 1950s

Boys	Girls
1. Michael	1. Mary
2. James	2. Linda
3. Robert	3. Patricia
4. John	4. Susan
5. David	5. Deborah
6. William	6. Barbara
7. Richard	7. Debra
8. Thomas	8. Karen
9. Frank	9. Nancy
10. Charles	10. Donna

top ten names of the 1960s

Boys	Girls
1. Michael	1. Lisa
2. David	2. Mary
3. John	3. Karen
4. James	4. Susan
5. Robert	5. Kimberly
6. Mark	6. Patricia
7. William	7. Linda
8. Richard	8. Donna
9. Thomas	9. Michelle
10. Jeffrey	10. Cynthia

top ten names of the 1970s

Boys	Girls
1. Michael	1. Jennifer
2. Christopher	2. Amy
3. Jason	3. Melissa
4. David	4. Michelle
5. James	5. Kimberly
6. John	6. Lisa
7. Robert	7. Angela
8. Brian	8. Heather
9. William	9. Stephanie
10. Matthew	10. Jessica

top ten names of the 1980s

Boys	Girls
1. Michael	1. Jessica
2. Christopher	2. Jennifer
3. Matthew	3. Amanda
4. Joshua	4. Ashley
5. David	5. Sarah
6. Daniel	6. Stephanie
7. James	7. Melissa
8. Robert	8. Nicole
9. John	9. Elizabeth
10. Joseph	10. Heather

top ten names of the 1990s

Boys	Girls
1. Michael	1. Ashley
2. Christopher	2. Jessica
3. Matthew	3. Emily
4. Joshua	4. Sarah
5. Jacob	5. Samantha
6. Andrew	6. Brittany
7. Daniel	7. Amanda
8. Nicholas	8. Elizabeth
9. Tyler	9. Taylor
10. Joseph	10. Megan

top ten names of the 2000s

Boys	Girls
1. Jacob	1. Emily
2. Michael	2. Hannah
3. Matthew	3. Madison
4. Joshua	4. Ashley
5. Christopher	5. Sarah
6. Nicholas	6. Alexis
7. Andrew	7. Samantha
8. Joseph	8. Jessica
9. Daniel	9. Taylor
10. Tyler	10. Elizabeth

top ten names of 2008

Boys	Girls
1. Jacob	1. Emily
2. Michael	2. Madison
3. Joshua	3. Hannah
4. Matthew	4. Emma
5. Andrew	5. Ashley
6. Christopher	6. Abigail
7. Joseph	7. Alexis
8. Daniel	8. Olivia
9. Nicholas	9. Samantha
10. Ethan	10. Sarah

Baby Names from around the Globe

names from u.s. cities and states

Boys:		Girls:	
Arlington	Austin	Alexandria	Atlanta
Boston	Dallas	Augusta	Charlotte
Denver	Jackson	Cheyenne	Dakota
Laramie	Montgomery	Florida	Georgia
Orlando	Reno	Helena	Madison
Roswell	Salem	Montana	Savannah
Sheridan			

popular hawaiian names

Boys:		Girls:	
Ailani	Kahoku	Akela	Alani
Kai	Kale	Aloha	Iolana
Kane	Keona	Keilana	Kiana
Makani	Meka	Leilani	Noelani
Palani		Oliana	Palila
		Roselani	

popular names in russia

Boys:		Girls:	
Aleksei	Arkadiy	Dasha	Galina
Feodor	Ilya	Irina	Lara
Kolya	Misha	Marina	Natalia
Nikolai	Pavel	Natasha	Oksana
Sacha	Sergei	Olga	Sofia
Vladilen	Yakov	Tatiana	Yelena

popular african-american names

Boys:		Girls:	
Deiondre	Denzel	Ananda	Beyonce
Deshawn	Dewayne	Latanya	Latisha
Jamar	Mykelti	Monisha	Nichelle
Roshaun	Shaquille	Shantell	Talisha
Taurean	Tyrell	Tamira	Taniel

popular korean names

Boys:

Chin	Chul
Chung-Ho	Hyun-Ki
Hyun-Su	Jin-Ho
Shin	Soo Sook
Suk	Sun
Yon	

Girls:

Cho	Eun
Hea	Hei
Hyun	Min
Sun	
Young	

popular names in scotland

Boys:

Lewis	Jack
Cameron	James
Kyle	Ryan
Ben	Callum
Matthew	Jamie

Girls:

Emma	Ellie
Amy	Sophie
Chloe	Erin
Rachel	Lucy
Lauren	Katie

popular muslim names

Boys:

Abdul	Ahmed
Habib	Hassan
Hussein	Jamal
Khalil	Omar
Mohammed	Salim
Youssef	Ziyad

Girls:

Aliya	Ayishah
Farah	Fatima
Jamila	Kalila
Leila	Malak
Rana	Samira
Suha	Yasmine

popular names in england

Boys:		Girls:	
Jack	Thomas	Chloe	Emily
James	Joshua	Megan	Charlotte
Daniel	Harry	Jessica	Lauren
Samuel	Joseph	Sophie	Olivia
Matthew	Callum	Hannah	Lucy

popular names in ireland

Boys:		Girls:	
Sean	Jack	Emma	Sarah
Adam	Conor	Aoife	Ciara
James	Daniel	Katie	Sophie
Michael	Cian	Rachel	Chloe
David	Dylan	Amy	Leah

popular names in poland

Boys:		Girls:	
Piotr	Jan	Anna	Maria
Andrzej	Krzysztof	Katarzyna	Malgorzata
Stanislaw	Tomasz	Agnieszka	Krystyna
Pawel	Jozef	Barbara	Ewa
Marcin	Marek	Ellbieta	Zofia

popular names in france

Boys:		Girls:	
Théo	Hugo	Léa	Chloé
Lucas	Thomas	Emma	Camille
Quentin	Alexandre	Manon	Sarah
Antoine	Maxime	Océane	Margaux
Valentin	Clément	Mathilde	Laura

popular names in the netherlands

Boys:		Girls:	
Daan	Sem	Emma	Anna
Thomas	Lars	Sanne	Iris
Milan	Thijs	Isa	Maud
Lucas	Bram	Lotte	Anouk
Jesse	Tim	Lisa	Julia

popular names in norway

Boys:		Girls:	
Mathias	Martin	Emma	Julie
Andreas	Jonas	Ida	Thea
Tobias	Daniel	Nora	Emilie
Sander	Magnus	Maria	Ingrid
Andrian	Henrik	Malin	Tuva

popular names in iceland

Boys:		Girls:	
Sigurdur	Gudmundur	Gudrun	Sigrídur
Jon	Gunnar	Kristín	Margret
Olafur	Magnus	Ingibjorg	Sigrun
Einar	Kristjan	Helga	Johanna
Bjorn	Bjarni	Anna	Ragnheidur

popular names in italy

Boys:		Girls:	
Giuseppe	Giovanni	Maria	Anna
Antonio	Mario	Giuseppina	Rosa
Luigi	Francesco	Angela	Giovanna
Angelo	Vincenzo	Teresa	Lucia
Pietro	Salvatore	Carmela	Caterina

african names

Boys:		Girls:	
Adisa	Amadi	Etana	Imani
Imamu	Jelani	Kamaria	Malaika
Kgosi	Mfalme	Morowa	Nafisa
Obataiye	Paki	Razina	Sanura
Sefu	Thabo	Thema	Zuri

popular names in chile

Boys:

Jose	Juan
Luis	Carlos
Jorge	Manuel
Victor	Francisco
Cristian	Pedro

Girls:

Maria	Ana
Rosa	Claudia
Patricia	Carolina
Camila	Daniela
Margarita	Juana

popular names in germany

Boys:

Maximilian	Alexander
Paul	Leon
Lukas	Luca
Felix	Jonas
Tim	David

Girls:

Marie	Sophie
Maria	Anna
Leonie	Leah
Laura	Lena
Katharina	Johanna

popular greek names

Boys:

Alexander	Aristotle
Constantine	Dimitri
Demos	Lucas
Nikos	Nicholas
Stefanos	Theo
Vasilis	

Girls:

Ariadne	Athena
Calista	Dimitria
Helena	Ionia
Katrina	Nia
Olga	Philana
Theodora	Zoe

popular chinese names

Boys:		Girls:	
An	Cheng	Ai	Bao
Ho	Hu	Chan	Dai
Jin	Kong	Hua	Jiao
Li	Liang	Jun	Li
Ning	Po	Lin	Ling
Qiang	Shing	Mei	Ping
Wen	Wing	Qian	Ting
Yong	Yu	Xian	Yan

popular hindu names

Boys:		Girls:	
Aditya	Arjun	Aditi	Chandi
Arnav	Dalal	Devi	Garesa
Hardeep	Nikhil	Maya	Natesa
Pranav	Rishi	Shreya	Sita
Rahul	Samir	Tara	Veda

popular names in spain

Boys:		Girls:	
Alejandro	Daniel	Lucia	Maria
Pablo	David	Paula	Laura
Javier	Adrian	Marta	Andrea
Alvaro	Sergio	Alba	Sara
Carlos	Hugo	Claudia	Ana

popular names in sweden

Boys:		Girls:	
William	Filip	Emma	Maja
Oscar	Lucas	Ida	Elin
Erik	Emil	Julia	Linnéa
Isak	Alexander	Hanna	Alva
Viktor	Anton	Wilma	Klara

popular names in japan

Boys:		Girls:	
Shun	Takumi	Misaki	Aoi
Shou	Ren	Nanami	Miu
Shouta	Souta	Riko	Miyu
Kaito	Kenta	Moe	Mitsuki
Daiki	Yuu	Yuuka	Rin

popular names in australia

Boys:		Girls:	
Jack	Joshua	Emily	Chloe
Lachan	Thomas	Olivia	Sophie
William	James	Jessica	Charlotte
Ethan	Samuel	Ella	Isabella
Daniel	Ryan	Sarah	Emma

Appendix E

Estimated Due Date Table

This chart lists due dates by month. Find the month and date on which your last menstrual period began, then look to see what your estimated due date is.

Date of Last Period. . . Your EDD		Date of Last Period. . . Your EDD	
1/1	10/8	2/4	11/11
1/2	10/9	2/5	11/12
1/3	10/10	2/6	11/13
1/4	10/11	2/7	11/14
1/5	10/12	2/8	11/15
1/6	10/13	2/9	11/16
1/7	10/14	2/10	11/17
1/8	10/15	2/11	11/18
1/9	10/16	2/12	11/19
1/10	10/17	2/13	11/20
1/11	10/18	2/14	11/21
1/12	10/19	2/15	11/22
1/13	10/20	2/16	11/23
1/14	10/21	2/17	11/24
1/15	10/22	2/18	11/25
1/16	10/23	2/19	11/26
1/17	10/24	2/20	11/27
1/18	10/25	2/21	11/28
1/19	10/26	2/22	11/29
1/20	10/27	2/23	11/30
1/21	10/28	2/24	12/1
1/22	10/29	2/25	12/2
1/23	10/30	2/26	12/3
1/24	10/31	2/27	12/4
1/25	11/1	2/28	12/5
1/26	11/2	3/1	12/6
1/27	11/3	3/2	12/7
1/28	11/4	3/3	12/8
1/29	11/5	3/4	12/9
1/30	11/6	3/5	12/10
1/31	11/7	3/6	12/11
2/1	11/8	3/7	12/12
2/2	11/9	3/8	12/13
2/3	11/10	3/9	12/14

Date of Last Period. . . Your EDD		Date of Last Period. . . Your EDD	
3/10	12/15	4/13	1/18
3/11	12/16	4/14	1/19
3/12	12/17	4/15	1/20
3/13	12/18	4/16	1/21
3/14	12/19	4/17	1/22
3/15	12/20	4/18	1/23
3/16	12/21	4/19	1/24
3/17	12/22	4/20	1/25
3/18	12/23	4/21	1/26
3/19	12/24	4/22	1/27
3/20	12/25	4/23	1/28
3/21	12/26	4/24	1/29
3/22	12/27	4/25	1/30
3/23	12/28	4/26	1/31
3/24	12/29	4/27	2/1
3/25	12/30	4/28	2/2
3/26	12/31	4/29	2/3
3/27	1/1	4/30	2/4
3/28	1/2	5/1	2/5
3/29	1/3	5/2	2/6
3/30	1/4	5/3	2/7
3/31	1/5	5/4	2/8
4/1	1/6	5/5	2/9
4/2	1/7	5/6	2/10
4/3	1/8	5/7	2/11
4/4	1/9	5/8	2/12
4/5	1/10	5/9	2/13
4/6	1/11	5/10	2/14
4/7	1/12	5/11	2/15
4/8	1/13	5/12	2/16
4/9	1/14	5/13	2/17
4/10	1/15	5/14	2/18
4/11	1/16	5/15	2/19
4/12	1/17	5/16	2/20

Date of Last Period. . . Your EDD   Date of Last Period. . . Your EDD

Date of Last Period	Your EDD	Date of Last Period	Your EDD
5/17	2/21	6/20	3/27
5/18	2/22	6/21	3/28
5/19	2/23	6/22	3/29
5/20	2/24	6/23	3/30
5/21	2/25	6/24	3/31
5/22	2/26	6/25	4/1
5/23	2/27	6/26	4/2
5/24	2/28	6/27	4/3
5/25	3/1	6/28	4/4
5/26	3/2	6/29	4/5
5/27	3/3	6/30	4/6
5/28	3/4	7/1	4/7
5/29	3/5	7/2	4/8
5/30	3/6	7/3	4/9
5/31	3/7	7/4	4/10
6/1	3/8	7/5	4/11
6/2	3/9	7/6	4/12
6/3	3/10	7/7	4/13
6/4	3/11	7/8	4/14
6/5	3/12	7/9	4/15
6/6	3/13	7/10	4/16
6/7	3/14	7/11	4/17
6/8	3/15	7/12	4/18
6/9	3/16	7/13	4/19
6/10	3/17	7/14	4/20
6/11	3/18	7/15	4/21
6/12	3/19	7/16	4/22
6/13	3/20	7/17	4/23
6/14	3/21	7/18	4/24
6/15	3/22	7/19	4/25
6/16	3/23	7/20	4/26
6/17	3/24	7/21	4/27
6/18	3/25	7/22	4/28
6/19	3/26	7/23	4/29

Date of Last Period. . . Your EDD		Date of Last Period. . . Your EDD	
7/24	4/30	8/27	6/3
7/25	5/1	8/28	6/4
7/26	5/2	8/29	6/5
7/27	5/3	8/30	6/6
7/28	5/4	8/31	6/7
7/29	5/5	9/1	6/8
7/30	5/6	9/2	6/9
7/31	5/7	9/3	6/10
8/1	5/8	9/4	6/11
8/2	5/9	9/5	6/12
8/3	5/10	9/6	6/13
8/4	5/11	9/7	6/14
8/5	5/12	9/8	6/15
8/6	5/13	9/9	6/16
8/7	5/14	9/10	6/17
8/8	5/15	9/11	6/18
8/9	5/16	9/12	6/19
8/10	5/17	9/13	6/20
8/11	5/18	9/14	6/21
8/12	5/19	9/15	6/22
8/13	5/20	9/16	6/23
8/14	5/21	9/17	6/24
8/15	5/22	9/18	6/25
8/16	5/23	9/19	6/26
8/17	5/24	9/20	6/27
8/18	5/25	9/21	6/28
8/19	5/26	9/22	6/29
8/20	5/27	9/23	6/30
8/21	5/28	9/24	7/1
8/22	5/29	9/25	7/2
8/23	5/30	9/26	7/3
8/24	5/31	9/27	7/4
8/25	6/1	9/28	7/5
8/26	6/2	9/29	7/6

Date of Last Period. . . Your EDD		Date of Last Period. . . Your EDD	
9/30	7/7	11/3	8/10
10/1	7/8	11/4	8/11
10/2	7/9	11/5	8/12
10/3	7/10	11/6	8/13
10/4	7/11	11/7	8/14
10/5	7/12	11/8	8/15
10/6	7/13	11/9	8/16
10/7	7/14	11/10	8/17
10/8	7/15	11/11	8/18
10/9	7/16	11/12	8/19
10/10	7/17	11/13	8/20
10/11	7/18	11/14	8/21
10/12	7/19	11/15	8/22
10/13	7/20	11/16	8/23
10/14	7/21	11/17	8/24
10/15	7/22	11/18	8/25
10/16	7/23	11/19	8/26
10/17	7/24	11/20	8/27
10/18	7/25	11/21	8/28
10/19	7/26	11/22	8/29
10/20	7/27	11/23	8/30
10/21	7/28	11/24	8/31
10/22	7/29	11/25	9/1
10/23	7/30	11/26	9/2
10/24	7/31	11/27	9/3
10/25	8/1	11/28	9/4
10/26	8/2	11/29	9/5
10/27	8/3	11/30	9/6
10/28	8/4	12/1	9/7
10/29	8/5	12/2	9/8
10/30	8/6	12/3	9/9
10/31	8/7	12/4	9/10
11/1	8/8	12/5	9/11
11/2	8/9	12/6	9/12

Date of Last Period. . . Your EDD

12/7 . . . . 9/13
12/8 . . . . 9/14
12/9 . . . . 9/15
12/10 . . . . 9/16
12/11 . . . . 9/17
12/12 . . . . 9/18
12/13 . . . . 9/19
12/14 . . . . 9/20
12/15 . . . . 9/21
12/16 . . . . 9/22
12/17 . . . . 9/23
12/18 . . . . 9/24
12/19 . . . . 9/25
12/20 . . . . 9/26
12/21 . . . . 9/27
12/22 . . . . 9/28
12/23 . . . . 9/29
12/24 . . . . 9/30
12/25 . . . . 10/1
12/26 . . . . 10/2
12/27 . . . . 10/3
12/28 . . . . 10/4
12/29 . . . . 10/5
12/30 . . . . 10/6
12/31 . . . . 10/7

Index